BEYOND THE THIRD DOOR

BASED ON A TRUE STORY

Maria Heckinger
8-22-19

BEYOND THE THIRD DOOR

BASED ON A TRUE STORY

MARIA HECKINGER

Front and back cover design by
Bryan Helfrich

First Edition 2019

ISBN: 978-1-54397-378-5 (print)

ISBN: 978-1-54397-379-2 (ebook)

This book is dedicated to
Ellen Pace and Hariklea Voukelatos
with love.

CONTENTS

WORDS FROM FRIENDS

In the early summer of 1956, feisty three-year-old Maria was put on a plane from Greece to New York. The long flight and frequent stops knocked out all the physical and mental energy that the little Greek girl had left, and she arrived sick and helpless at the other end. Until then and for many more years to come, all life-changing decisions were made for her. But Maria took back agency, traveled back to Greece and reconnected with her biological family in Patras. The moving and occasionally humorous story of becoming a well-rounded, mature individual with a completed identity had to be told, and it had to be told by the person who lived it and retook charge of her life and quest. Maria's book speaks in her own unique voice to the many issues of the adoptee identity interrupted. Her book opens up a dialogue for and with all those who have experienced something similar but may not yet have found the words--or may not yet have embarked on the adventure of the quest. As a researcher studying the Greek postwar adoptions, I welcome Maria's rich and courageous testimony wholeheartedly and encourage others to follow her path.

Professor Gonda Van Steen, Koraes Chair of Modern Greek and Byzantine History, Language and Literature, King's College London, author of *Adoption, Memory, and Cold War Greece: Kid pro quo?* (University of Michigan Press, 2019).

Half a continent separates us now, but there was a time when Maria and I were mere yards apart. I have known her all my life, but I didn't realize it until our paths crossed nearly 62 years later. Maria and I were orphans together in the Patras Municipal Orphanage that created a bond that may get lost but is never broken. Her story is my story; it is the story of some 3,500 other Greek orphans from the 1950s and 60s. Before I started my search, I thought I was alone. Maria's courage to tell her story lets us know we are not alone and gives hope to those of us still searching. It is good to have reconnected with my friend.

Merrill Jenkins, Patras adoptee

Maria Heckinger is a force of nature with a heartwarming story so miraculous that it would not seem out-of-place in a work of fiction. I had the great privilege of watching as her manuscript developed over time in my memoir writing class, and the great joy of editing an earlier version of it. You will be heartbroken to learn the story of young Hariklea, a girl whose station in Greek society led to her being powerless as the most crucial decision of one's life was made on her behalf. You will be captivated by Maria's anguish, heroism, and perseverance as she searches for answers regarding the circumstances of her birth. You will be inspired by her journey from despair to peace and understanding. Maria Heckinger's story will give hope to those adopted children and birth mothers who live with an ongoing sense of loss.

Christopher Luna, Editor, Writing Coach and Co-Founder of Printed Matter Vancouver/ Memoir Writing Instructor

SO MANY THANK YOU'S

My husband Matthew whose encouragement and patience is limitless

Brothers Michael and Richard Jr. for making family a priority

Matt's sons and daughter-in-law who bring me so much joy

Sister Katina for loving me as a sister

Greek uncles, aunts, and cousins who welcomed me with open arms, and open hearts

Greek Priests: George Savvas, Tom Tsagalakis, Paul Kaplanis and his wife, Evi

His Eminence Gabriel from Turkey

My friend Bev who became part of my Greek family

And…In coming full circle, I'd like to give a big thank you to the people who brought me to this page in my life story.

Friends and family in San Diego, CA., and Vancouver, WA.

The Campus Lab School Class of 1965

MARIA HECKINGER

The First Methodist Church of La Mesa, CA

Helix High School Class of 1971

To all my fellow Greek adoptees who share my heart

Friends and educators of the Vancouver Public Schools during my 31-year career

Fellow literary friends from Clark County's vibrant writing scene.

My friends at Holy Trinity Greek Orthodox Cathedral of Portland, Oregon who support me spiritually

Gonda, my friend, and expert on all things Greek

My writing instructor Christopher

Wise editors and kind readers: Toni, Lynn, Melanie, Matt, Gonda, Robert, Cindy

Photo editor: Jonathan

A NOTE FROM THE AUTHOR

The three voices in this story include two mothers living on opposite sides of the planet, whose lives and loves connected them to the same child. Each woman lived with shame: Hariklea Voukelatos because she had a child, and Ellen Pace because she could not.

I am the third voice, which was pieced together over 44 years, using journals I kept while visiting Greece, Ellen's scrapbook, and Hariklea's oral history. I have chosen to write this story entirely in the first-person, allowing each woman to speak her truth.

It may make you wonder: can anyone choose their parents, or do they choose you?

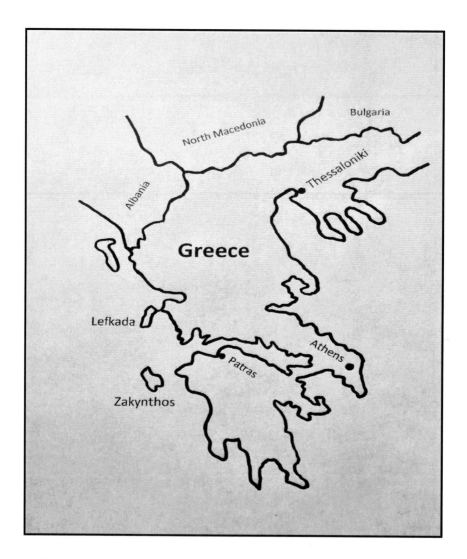

The island of Lefkada is located off the western coast of Greece and connected by a causeway to the mainland.

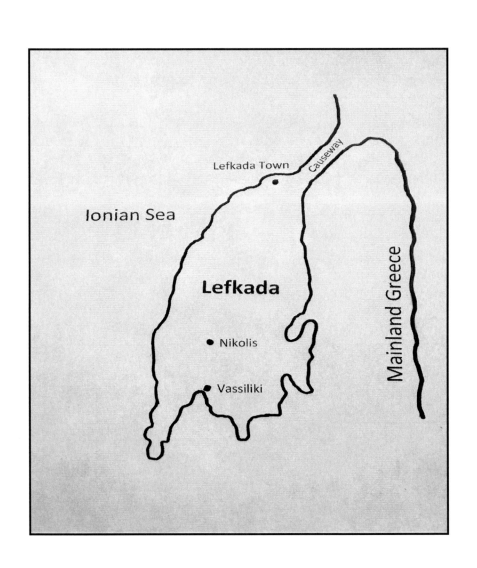

HARIKLEA'S STORY

MY SMALL WINDOW ON THE SEA

A WARM BREEZE BLOWS ACROSS THE GREEK ISLAND OF Lefkada as I dry the morning dishes. Staring out of the tiny kitchen window of the house that had been in my family for generations, I know I'll never tire of that view. Geraniums in pink, white, and red bask in the sun as they spill over the old olive cans and red clay pots bordering the patio. Grape vines twist and snake overhead to form a cool, shady cover over the arbor next to the house. Garlic braids drape the beams and oregano dries on the fence nearby. The music for the day comes from an ancient olive tree that stands guard like a sentinel and is home to hundreds of cicadas.

With the last dish from the morning meal on the drying rack, I move into the living room to dust. This family area is my favorite because it brings back memories of Zoe, my Mama. Icons and photos sit on the mantle above the fireplace. Hand embroidered doilies and a table runner added the finishing touches to the table and sofa. Mama

1

Zoe and I had spent many hours cooking meals in the stone fireplace and warming our toes on the hearth. The brightly colored, woven rug completed the room. Hand-woven by Mama, I think of her every time I see it.

The world has long read of Greek tragedies, but I, Hariklea Voukelatos, have lived one. My Mama, Zoe, was killed in a senseless act of rage by my Baba, Efstathios, when I was just six-years-old. In those days, marriages were arranged, dowries were paid, and men *owned* their wives. Husbands were free to punish them as they saw fit, even if it resulted in death. The following year, 1945, brought more heartache. I contracted polio and spent weeks in bed. The women of the village nursed me back to health, but I was left with a withered ankle that rendered my foot useless. Now I limp and hobble around on a three-inch thick rubber-soled shoe and use a wooden cane. I was shocked and dismayed over what the disease had done to me. There was nothing easy about living in a mountain village with polio.

Like most of the poorest village girls, I was not allowed to attend school, so I never learned to read or write. The men were afraid if we learned those skills, we would spend our time writing to boys. It was a ridiculous and unfair custom, but I could do nothing. I am now 15 years old with no girlfriends, only my two cousins. I spend most of my time alone and know nothing of the world beyond my island of Lefkada, and my small window on the sea.

I run the household for four men: Baba, and three brothers, Thodoris, Nikos and Dimitri. As I set about making *moussaka* for the midday meal, I wondered if my only purpose in life is to cook and clean. I so wished I could have shared the morning chores with Mama. It has been nine years since her death, and I still miss her terribly. With the men tending the olive trees, the village is quiet, and I can sing the songs my mother taught me.

While working away, singing softly to myself, I was startled by an approaching shadow. I was not expecting anyone. If Baba was returning early, then something was wrong. The front door inched open, and I was surprised to see the face of a man I knew well, Yiorgos Doxaras, Baba's best friend. He was in his 30's and lived a few houses up the road with his wife and five young children. Yiorgos and Baba were also business partners. They bought an olive press and supported their families by selling the oil from the village trees. Alarm bells went off in my head as he stepped inside and closed the door behind him, slowly, deliberately.

"Yiorgos, what's wrong?" I asked. "Shouldn't you be at work tending the olives?" Ignoring the question, Yiorgos sneered at me, "I have watched you grow into a beautiful, young woman Hariklea. It's too bad you are a cripple. No man will want you, so I'm going to do you a favor."

I took a few steps back as the glint in his eyes told me I was in trouble. "You're not supposed to be here, Yiorgos. You need to leave right now."

He said nothing but reached out and grabbed me by the arm. I was no match for his crushing grip. I shouted, but he placed his hand over my mouth to muffle my screams. I tried to bite him, but the sharp sting of a slap across my face stopped me. With his free arm, he dragged me to the living room carpet and pushed me down. He lifted my dress, pulled down my underwear, and there on the floor of the only safe place I knew, he hurt me. The pain between my legs was sharp and immediate, and I did not understand what was happening to me. The weight of his body on top of mine made it hard to breathe, and the acrid smell of his sweat made me wretch. I begged him to stop, but he did not. It was over in an instant. Lying there, shocked, sore, and confused, I stared at the ceiling until my tears dried, and my breathing returned to normal. I continued to lay there and think of Mama. Growing up without a mother, I knew nothing of womanhood but realized something dreadful had happened to me. Aching all over, I stood up and realized I was alone. Yiorgos had slipped out of the house like nothing had happened.

I pulled up my underwear, rearranged my disheveled dress, and made my way to the kitchen sink where I put a cool cloth to my throbbing cheek. Why like a thief had Yiorgos returned to the village to hurt me? Our families were friends who spent many years together. His last words still rang in my ears. What had he meant when he said he was "doing me a favor?" I felt utterly lost. If Mama Zoe were here, she would have explained what Yiorgos had done and know what to do. If Mama were here, this would not have happened. Sobbing, I crawled on hands and knees upstairs to my bedroom where I collapsed on my bed and fell into a fitful sleep.

The midday sun streaming into the bedroom woke me up and reminded me I could not lay there much longer. I had to compose myself before the men returned home for the midday meal. I got up, changed my clothes, and headed downstairs to the kitchen where the day had begun with such a sunny start. While finishing the *moussaka*, I thought about what to do next. I wanted to tell somebody about Yiorgos but knew no one would believe me, a simple village girl. It was safest to keep the incident a secret, especially from Baba. If he found out what had happened, it might cost me my life.

The death of Mama taught me men's violent behavior was accepted, and women just endured it. When I was six, I saw Baba beat her to death with a wooden club. It happened during WWII when the Italian army occupied Lefkada. The soldiers raided the shops, took all the food and livestock they could get their hands on, and left the villagers to starve. The only food we had was what we grew or raised on our property. All the livestock was kept at home, away from the soldiers hungry for meat. Efstathios, my Baba, had warned Mama Zoe not to take the goats out to graze because the soldiers were everywhere, and they might steal one. She did not listen to him and took them out to pasture anyway. An Italian soldier spied the tiny woman and her small herd and stole one. Zoe had disobeyed her husband and would suffer the consequences. Her fear turned to panic as she returned to the village short one goat.

I can still remember the panic in Mama's eyes as Baba grabbed the wooden cudgel; he used to beat her. He looked crazed as he swung the club at her with full force. It made a sickening thud as it tore Zoe's flesh and broke her bones. I screamed at Baba to stop. Despite my protests, he kept hitting her until she fell to the ground in a bloody heap. I thought he would finally stop, yet to my horror, the beating continued until she stopped moving. Mama did not die right away but lingered in unbearable pain for two days. If Baba had treated his wife and the mother of his children this way, what would he do to me if he learned the truth?

Around noon Baba and my brothers returned from the orchards. I'm not sure how I found the strength to continue and serve lunch as if nothing happened. If they noticed anything different about me, they said nothing. I managed to get through that day and the next, but life wasn't easy. Nikolis was a small village, and our family crossed paths with Yiorgos nearly every day. On days when I had to draw water from the communal well, I planned my trips carefully so I would be alone.

Meanwhile, Yiorgos continued to run the olive oil business with Baba as if nothing had happened. He did not seek me out again, but an emotional numbness came over me as the days turned into weeks. I was depressed and had trouble sleeping. I considered sharing my troubles with my Aunt Fotini. Married to Baba's brother, she was 35 years old, had a family of her own, and lived just around the corner. She had witnessed Mama's beating and cared for her until she died. Fotini was as close to a mother as I would know, but I did not confide in her either. It was too dangerous to trust anyone in the village.

Winter arrived bringing inclement weather that gave me an excuse to stay inside and avoid Yiorgos. As I fell back into the routine of caring for Baba and my brothers, I realized something was wrong. My stomach was swollen, and I was exhausted all the time. I knew about cysts and tumors from other villagers who had experienced them. That had to be what was wrong with me. I was young and naïve but knew two things: I needed a doctor, and I was terrified!

BETRAYAL

IT WAS A BRIGHT, CRISP SATURDAY IN NIKOLIS. FEBRUARY was loosening its wintery grip, and spring was just around the corner. Almost seven months had passed since Yiorgos had hurt me, and something was wrong! Both my belly and my fears had grown each month since that day. When I dared to venture outside, I hid my body under loose-fitting dresses and bulky sweaters, but it did not stop the villagers' whisperings and sideways glances. Desperate, I reluctantly turned to Aunt Fotini for help. Gathering my courage, I walked to her home and found her in the kitchen slicing eggplant. Quietly, I told her I needed her advice and was relieved when she agreed to listen.

With coffees in hand, I took a deep breath and tried to speak but burst into tears before I uttered a word. Fotini wrapped me in her arms and stroked my hair until, in between sobs, I revealed my secret. We sipped our drinks and sat arm in arm long after I finished, letting the silence soothe us. At last Fotini spoke, "I'm not sure if Yiorgos caused the... tumor, but you should ask for his help first. If he refuses, you must tell Baba what he did."

I wondered if Fotini knew more than she'd let on, but I trusted her. Taking her advice, I waited to find Yiorgos alone. I had not spoken to him since that day in August, and the prospect of facing him filled me with dread. A few days later, I got my chance when he was having coffee in the village square. I approached him quietly and whispered, "Yiorgos, I am sick, and I need a doctor. Something is growing in my belly, and I hope you will help me. I am asking you before I have to tell Baba."

Yiorgos spat back, "I have no help for you, a cripple. I don't want you, and no one else will either. I owe you nothing."

He turned his back on me and returned to his coffee as I stood there in stunned silence. I was not expecting such a curt and cold-hearted rejection. Yiorgos was callous and ruthless, and I was foolish to think he would help me. Feeling desperate and alone, I trudged home to tell Fotini about Yiorgos' heartless response. She expressed her disappointment but reminded me I had no choice left. I had to tell Baba. Still reeling from Yiorgos' cruelty, and afraid of telling Baba, I needed time to think. I would talk to him tomorrow.

Fear was my only companion as I fed the animals, prepared the bread for the morning meal, and cooked dinner for Baba and my brothers. I ate in silence as my mind raced with thoughts of how to tell him what Yiorgos had done. Upstairs in my room, tormented with thoughts of Baba, I could not sleep. *Family honor is everything to him. Will he help me or kill me like Mama? Will he take me to a doctor? What will he do when he learned the truth about his best friend?*

The next morning, I was exhausted and panic-stricken. While preparing breakfast, I saw several villagers had gathered up the street at Yiorgos' house. I listened to the loud chatter and heard someone say Yiorgos had left Nikolis last night without a word to anyone. Wearing just the clothes on his back, and carrying a bag of food, he left behind his wife, five children, and a business. I was puzzled and troubled by his behavior. *Why had Yiorgos left so suddenly? Did this have something to do with me? What would happen to his family?*

Baba came down to breakfast, and I could no longer delay talking to him. My brothers would be up soon, so it was now or never. Sitting at the kitchen table, it took every ounce of courage I had to tell Baba what Yiorgos had done to me. I wasn't even sure how to describe his actions, but I did my best. When I finished, I asked him to take me to see a doctor. He looked me over and replied, "I have noticed the changes in you and seen the neighbors' looks when you leave the house, but I didn't think anything was wrong. You are maturing from a girl into a young woman. I just thought you were eating more." I sat there too scared to speak; he wasn't finished with me yet.

Watching Baba, a change overcome him. Like a pot of water coming to a boil, his anger roiled, and his breathing sped up as he realized what had happened right under his roof. Baba jumped up, pounded his fist on the table without a word, and marched out of the house up the street. I knew he had one thing on his mind; kill Yiorgos!

From the kitchen window, I recognized Baba's posture as I saw him talking with the neighbors in front of Yiorgos' house. His screams echoed down the valley when he learned his best friend had fled the island like a coward under cover of night, never to return. Baba's world had turned upside down with the events of the last 24 hours, and he was angry. I don't know where he went, but it was hours before I saw him walking back home. Strangely, he no longer looked mad, but instead appeared calm and thoughtful. Baba's changed demeanor terrified me even more. My panic grew with each step he took.

Efstathios yanked open the front door and bellowed, "Hariklea, go upstairs and pack your clothes. You and Eleni (my cousin) are leaving for Patras tomorrow on the first bus. You will stay with my sister, Dora, and see a doctor about your tumor." Baba turned abruptly and marched back out of the house. Standing there frozen, it took me a minute to understand his directions. He had spared my life and agreed to let me see a doctor, a response I was not expecting. Perhaps killing me, his child, was too extreme even for him. Whatever his reason, I thanked God I was not going to suffer the same fate as Mama.

Upstairs in my room, I was sure I'd be returning soon after seeing the doctor, so I packed lightly. My older brother, Thodoris, heard the commotion and came upstairs. He noticed the open suitcase and asked about it. We were close, so I told him where I was going and why. Relieved he did not press me for details; I assured him I would be back in a few days. We parted ways at the top of the stairs, and I finished packing. Tomorrow would be a long day.

ELEKTRA

THE MORNING SUN WAS A SLIVER ON THE HORIZON AS I grabbed my suitcase and headed downstairs. I found bus money on the kitchen table, but no friends or family to see me off or wish me well. Hurt but not surprised, I grabbed the cash, a snack for the trip, and met Eleni on the road where we walked to the bus stop in silence. I was relieved about seeing a doctor but scared of leaving Lefkada. I had no idea what awaited me in Patras.

The bus arrived on time and began its slow, winding, descent out of the mountains. I had ridden a bus before to attend the children's carnival in Lefkas Town but had never left the island. The sharp turns made me sick to my stomach, so I leaned out the window, gulped in the fresh air, and willed myself not to throw up. Just in time, the road straightened out, and I began to feel better. We drove south along the coast and over the causeway connecting Lefkada to the mainland of Greece. Looking back at my island home as it faded in the distance, I thought of my family and worried how long it would be until my return.

The drive to Patras would take most of the day, so we settled in, had a bite, and took in the scenery. Three years older than me, at 18, cousin Eleni was a sensitive girl who didn't pry about the reason for the trip and was good company. She had visited Patras before, but this was my first trip, so everything looked new to me. Eleni did her best to point out the sights and answer my non-stop questions. Quaint towns, calm lakes, and miles of farmland made up most of the scenery. Old trucks loaded with too many watermelons or tomatoes spewed black exhaust as they made their way to the markets.

My biggest shock came as we approached Patras, a city I had only seen on the television. Those images did not prepare me for the cars, roads, and buildings that seemed to go on forever. The noise of Patras was unlike anything I had ever heard. The sidewalks were crowded with people talking, laughing, and shouting as they went about their daily business. Drivers sped along full streets honking their horns, daring anyone to step in their way. Shops, coffee houses, and restaurants filled every corner. I was both mesmerized and intimidated by the enormity of it all!

Exhausted and hungry, we pulled into the Patras station where Eleni found a horse cab that took us to Aunt Dora's house. As she opened the door, she greeted Eleni warmly but did not hide her scorn for me. Right then, I learned family honor on the islands extended to the mainland relatives as well. Eleni and I settled into our room and joined Dora in the kitchen for a bowl of warm *avgolemono* soup, salad, and bread. It was a delicious way to end a long day, but the trip had taken its toll. I thanked Dora for her hospitality and went to bed early, leaving Eleni to fend for herself with my aunt. As my head hit the pillow, I felt hopeful tomorrow would bring me some answers.

Morning arrived. After a quick breakfast, Eleni and I began the walk to the doctor's office. Patras was nothing like sleepy little Nikolis in the morning. The noise and pace of this big city was a shock to my senses. Everywhere I looked, I saw, smelled, or heard something new. I was still in a daze as we arrived and knocked on the doctor's door. A middle-aged woman who insisted we call her Elektra answered the door. Portly with short black hair, she wore well-worn shoes and a faded dress under her threadbare lab coat. Elektra's maternal demeanor and warm smile helped put me at ease. She ushered me into an exam room where I changed into a strange-looking gown that tied in the back. Feeling ever so exposed, I sat on the exam table until Elektra entered and asked me how she could help. I answered, "Something is wrong with my stomach. It has been growing for the past few months. I am worried I may have a tumor." She suggested an examination.

Elektra helped me onto my back, placed each foot in a cold steel loop, and began her examination. Reassuring and gentle, she talked me through every step of the exam; but that did not lessen my humiliation over being so visible and touched in such private places. When she finished, the results took my breath away. I did not have a tumor at all; I was seven months pregnant. Things started to make sense now. A baby explained my growing figure, the murmurs, and glances from the villagers, and why Yiorgos had left the island so hastily.

I was 15 and did not want a baby, so I asked Elektra to get rid of it. When she said it was too late to terminate the pregnancy, I broke down and sobbed. Pregnant, with no husband, Yiorgos had ruined my life. I bawled as Elektra rubbed my back and tried to console me. As my wails softened to whimpers, the doctor told me she had a possible solution, but there were a couple of conditions.

First, she would have the "womanhood" talk with me. I quickly agreed, anything to make this go away. Elektra described the physical changes girls went through as they became women in a way I could understand. I turned beet red when she explained sex and conception. The thought of a man and woman doing *that* was unthinkable and frightening to me. When Elektra added, adults often did *that* for enjoyment, I almost fainted. Despite my fear and unease, I was thankful Elektra had stepped into the role of a mother and told me the things I should have learned from Mama.

Elektra's discovery my hymen was still partially attached was a rare, but not unheard of, condition that provided her a possible solution to my dilemma. She would diagnose me with a stomach ailment and require I stay in Patras for treatment. I would carry the baby to term, at which point Elektra would deliver it by Caesarian section and put it up for adoption. After the delivery, she would stitch my hymen back into place so I could remain a virgin, save face, and return home.

Elektra's other condition was my age. Because I was only 16, she could do nothing without Baba's permission. When she asked about calling him, I begged her to call right away because it might take a while to get him to the telephone. Nikolis had only one phone located in the market. I prayed the store was open so the owner could answer. When a villager got a phone call, he would send a child to the recipient's home or stand outside the store and yell down the hill at the top of his lungs. I breathed a sigh of relief. Surely Baba would agree to such a plan.

Eleni and I waited anxiously outside Elektra's office for news from Nikolis. An hour passed before Elektra appeared and ushered me into her office to explain Baba had not agreed to her solution. She said he made his feelings about me brutally clear. "The entire village knows you are pregnant with Yiorgos' child. They want nothing to do with you or the baby. You have disgraced your family and ruined another. You are disowned and can never return home."

I sat in shocked silence as Elektra's words sank in. Baba had spared my life; but his decision meant I would never see my brothers, my cousins, or my home again. Paralyzed with fear, I could barely breathe. Now there was no need to perform a Cesarean section; I could give birth naturally. After the delivery, keeping the child, or putting it up for adoption was something only I could decide. I saw only despair ahead.

Since there was nothing more Elektra could do right now, I needed to return to my aunt's home to think. It took all of Elektra's and Eleni's strength to stand me up and help me out of the office. Moving along the street in shock, I had no memory of walking back to my aunt's house. Opening the door, the smirk on Dora's face revealed she had known the truth. She didn't react at all when I told her I was pregnant. I should have kept quiet, but against my better judgment, I mentioned Elektra's solution and Baba's response. Dora nodded and heartlessly added, "I knew you were pregnant. Now you must live on the streets with prostitutes and gypsies because you are no better than them. You can spend one night here, but you must leave in the morning. I am at risk of being shunned for even helping you in your shameful condition."

With that, Dora abruptly turned and went into the kitchen to serve the afternoon meal. I ate in silence while she and Eleni exchanged the latest news from Patras and Nikolis. I was envious as they discussed their plans, something I no longer had. Tears streamed down my cheeks and salted my food as I helped myself to extra portions of chicken and potatoes. I didn't know when I'd get to eat again.

The last two days had taken a terrible toll on me, so I excused myself and went to the bedroom to rest. Lying there I realized tonight would be my last night in a real bed.

THE STREETS

UP EARLY THE NEXT MORNING, ELENI AND I PACKED AND joined Aunt Dora for a light breakfast of coffee and bread with honey. Filled with dread over what lay ahead, I didn't feel much like talking. We thanked Dora for her compassion and headed for the door. I expected her to launch into a farewell tirade about my condition, but she surprised me with a gesture of sympathy. She gave me a sack of left-over chicken and bread, a blanket, and a few drachmas. It was a kind thing to do, and I thanked her, but there was no reply as she turned away and slowly shut the door behind me.

Now it was just Eleni and me on the porch, and it was time to say goodbye. We held each other and cried as we realized we might never see each other again. She was returning to Nikolis today. I knew Eleni was worried about me, but she couldn't help either, Efstathios' word was law. I wanted to hold on to her forever, but eventually, she whispered, "May God protect you and keep you safe," kissed my cheeks, and set out for the bus station. I waved, but she did not look back at me, not even once.

BEYOND THE THIRD DOOR

It was March of 1953 when I left Dora's house and walked down the street to a bench where I could sit and think. Last week I was home in my village making dinner, keeping house, and watching over my brothers. Now I was on the streets with nothing but a cheap suitcase and a blanket. Cast out by my Nikolis and Patras family; I had no idea how to take care of myself or stay out of harm's way. With no money, no place to sleep, and no idea where my next meal would come from; I was overwhelmed with fear. I sat there a long time trying to figure out what to do next. The truth was my condition and inability to read and write left me with no options. Baba's sister was right; I would have to beg on the streets like the gypsies and the prostitutes I feared.

My immediate concern was food, as the kicking child in my belly was a continual reminder; I was eating for two. I ate Dora's chicken and set out to get my bearings. This city was so big I felt like it could swallow me up and no one would miss me. Using my cane and carrying only a blanket and a suitcase, I was a pathetic sight as I limped up and down the steep streets. I was huge, my feet were too swollen to wear shoes, and I felt like no one cared if I lived or died. I walked until I found a corner that looked like a suitable place to stop, but there was nowhere to sit. Bringing my suitcase had been a good idea because it made a decent seat and kept me off the filthy, cold pavement. As I sat there wrapped in my blanket with my head in my hands, a man walked by and dropped a coin at my feet. Picking it up, I rubbed it between my fingers to feel if it was real. That coin was another painful reminder of how tragic my life had become, but also how I could survive. I decided to stay put and see what the day would bring. Most passers-by eyed me with contempt. Some hurled insults, but a few took pity and gave me money or food.

It wasn't long before another concern arose; I needed a bathroom. With no idea where to go, I asked and was directed to one of the public restrooms. Smelling it before I saw it, I took a big gulp of air, held my breath, and finished as quickly as possible. Right then, I decided to use public bathrooms only when necessary. I could wash up using water from the fountains, and shrubs would be adequate for my other needs.

As the sun set, I considered my next problem, finding a safe and dry place to spend the night. I was too frightened to trust anyone, so I looked for a location where I could sleep alone. I wandered around until I found a well-lit park bench. Scanning the area for anyone who looked suspicious, I wrapped myself in the blanket, placed my suitcase at one end for a headrest, and laid down. It made a terrible pillow, and the solid, wooden, slats dug into my hips and back. The thin blanket did little to keep out the cold, and my stomach complained constantly.

In a strange twist, the lamp I thought would keep me safe also attracted thousands of bugs, insects, and other creatures. Miserably uncomfortable and filled with fear, I drifted in and out of restless sleep. I was dozing off again when the voices of people starting their day woke me. Sitting up, I pulled myself together as best I could and began my search for a new corner. Breakfast today was a stale slice of Dora's bread and a half-eaten piece of fruit. It wasn't much, but I was relieved to have survived my first night on the streets of Patras.

One miserable day blended into the next as I fell into a routine of begging for food by day and finding a different place to sleep each night. My utter disbelief at the turn my life had taken almost crushed my will to live. The only thing keeping me going was my innocent baby and the realization we needed each other to survive.

Tavern owners took pity and gave me table scraps when I begged at their backdoors. Spoiled fruits and vegetables were often available in the alleys behind the markets. Nights were the worst because they brought cold and fear, along with despair. When it rained, I found an abandoned building or a covered doorway, but sleeping on the cold, hard stone was next to impossible. Even the park benches, as bad as they were, made better beds.

BEYOND THE THIRD DOOR

After more nights on the street than I cared to remember fortune finally smiled on me. One afternoon a young woman pushing a stroller sat down next to me in the park. She was on her way home and stopped to rest. We talked, and she was shocked to learn I was homeless. Surely an angel, she offered to help and led me to the home of a merciful priest. He fed me simple food that, for a moment, eased my gnawing hunger. He also found me a safe place to spend the night near his church. It was an empty shed really, but he put down an old mattress, so I would be safe and protected from the weather. My days were still spent searching and begging for food, but it was a huge relief to know I had a secure place to sleep at night.

One evening the priest stopped by the shed and announced he had found me a job as a live-in domestic for a family in his parish. I started work the next day, but my joy and relief were short-lived when it became clear I would be no more than an indentured servant. My employers worked me relentlessly, fed me little, and paid me nothing. I endured daily ridicule, cursing, and self-righteous scolding for my condition. They didn't even give me a real bed to sleep on, only a long cushion salvaged from the trash. This situation continued for several weeks until I could last no more and passed out on the kitchen floor.

I spent a week in the hospital for exhaustion and malnutrition. My stay was a much-needed reprieve from the rigors of my life. Finally, I had enough to eat, a clean bed to sleep in, and medical care appropriate for a pregnant girl. Lying there, I had lots of time to think. Elektra had explained I was pregnant because of a *rape*. I didn't even know there was a word for what Yiorgos had done to me. I just knew he had ruined my life, and I was going to be a mother at 16. Would I be able to love and care for this child, or would I blame it for my current situation and give it up for adoption? Only time could answer that question.

During my hospital stay, I met Aglaia Messini. She became my best friend and the mentor I so desperately needed. Until a few months ago, Baba had made every decision in my life. Alone and 16 years old, I was still too young to make such adult decisions on my own. Another angel, Aglaia, stepped into the role of protector and advisor. At 33, she was twice my age and radiated compassion and wisdom. She was a hard worker who held down two cleaning jobs to make ends meet: one in the hospital where I met her and the other in the Patras orphanage. Her husband had survived the horrific battles of World War II, only to be killed during Greece's Civil War (1946-1949). Now she lived alone in the home she had shared with him.

Upon my release from the hospital, Aglaia arranged for me to work as a domestic for friends of hers. This time I had a bed, food to eat, and no judgments about my condition. The days were still long and challenging, but I was grateful for the job.

Spring finally arrived, bringing blue skies and ocean breezes. It was April, and I was in my final month of pregnancy. Work as a domestic was becoming more and more grueling, and I could barely complete the household chores. My back and legs hurt all the time, and I was long past being able to bend over. Tired of being pregnant, tired of working long hours, and tired of being hungry, I was just... plain... tired.

BABY MARIA

ON THE MORNING OF MAY 3ᴿᴰ, 1953, WHILE SWEEPING THE front porch, my water broke. I wasn't sure what had happened, but soon, the contractions started, and I knew the baby was coming. Oh, how I missed my Mama. If she hadn't died so young, I would have known what to expect. At the hospital, I was whisked into a room and placed on a bed with the same metal loops I had seen in Elektra's office. The nurse lifted my legs in place, and within minutes, a young doctor arrived. I feared he might mistreat me because of my condition, but his quiet, self-assured, manner calmed me. If he knew about my situation, he said nothing.

After examining me, the doctor announced it was time to start pushing. As the contractions intensified, I screamed and thought I would die from the pain. Somewhere, amidst all the activity, a nurse yelled, "Breathe, now push, breathe, now push." The nurses pushed on my stomach for hours until I gave birth to a baby girl. There was blood everywhere, which frightened me. Bone-tired and sore, I worried for a moment until her first wail startled everyone in the room. I breathed a huge sigh of relief as Maria Voukelatos announced her arrival.

A nurse cleaned her and placed Maria in my arms. In an instant, my world changed forever. Every doubt and fear about my ability to love this child vanished. It was love at first sight! My heart filled with such joy I thought it would burst. From her shiny eyes to her stubby little toes, she was perfect. Stroking her soft, buttery cheek, I realized I was part of something larger than myself. I was a mother who would do anything to protect my child.

The doctor stopped by later and checked on Maria but told me I was not going home yet. When the nurses pushed on me during labor, they'd caused internal damage, so I had to stay in the hospital at least a week to recover. He also informed me I would not be able to give birth naturally again; a cesarean section was now my only choice. The irony of his statement was not lost on me as I remembered Elektra's plan to help me. Another baby was the last thing I worried about, so I put it out of my mind.

After a week, the nurses showed me how to wean her off breast milk with "chi" (tea and sugar water), as was the Greek custom. Soon I would be leaving the hospital and going to Aglaia's house. My dear friend had offered Maria and me her spare bedroom until I could figure things out. Once again, God showed himself to me through the mercy of Aglaia. If not for her, I would have been homeless once again.

During my time in the hospital, two significant events took place: Maria's baptism and an introduction to Mrs. Karras, a local business owner. Under normal conditions, baptisms take place after a baby is at least 40 days old, but I couldn't wait that long. There was a small church in the hospital, Saint Charalambos, and a priest who agreed to perform the ceremony. On May 12th, Maria Voukelatos was baptized in the Orthodox Christian faith with Aglaia happily serving as the *Nouna* (Godmother). I named her "Maria" after the Virgin Mary, in hope, the mother of Christ would protect my baby girl.

Mrs. Karras, a long-time friend of Aglaia, was in the hospital room next door. She was worldly-wise and kind so whenever possible I would take Maria and visit. We became friends, and I grew to trust her. Gradually I revealed what had brought me to this point in my life. I told her about Nikolis, Elektra's proposed solution, and the nightmare of life on the streets. Mrs. Karras did not condemn Baba's actions but took pity and offered me a cleaning job in her furniture factory. Her offer would change my life profoundly.

Maria and I left the hospital shortly after the baptism and followed Aglaia to her home. From the hospital, Aglaia had scavenged baby blankets, formula, diapers, and a washtub that made an excellent crib. We spent the rest of the day holding, feeding, and just looking at Maria. She slept most of the time, but when she was awake, her little arms and legs wiggled in every direction as she took in her surroundings. Her giggle bubbles made me laugh, and when she grabbed my little finger with her hand, I cried tears of joy.

As happy as I was to be safe at home with my baby, I was anxious about what lay ahead. Living on the streets with a baby was not an option. I needed to work. On the other hand, the chances of anyone hiring an illiterate cripple were small. It seemed there was no acceptable answer. Over dinner, I shared my troubles with Aglaia, who listened but did not seem to hear me. I didn't know if she was tired or preoccupied so I took Maria and went to bed.

Over breakfast the next morning, Aglaia was still not herself, so I asked what was wrong. Her eyes brimmed with tears as she revealed she had been up most of the night trying to come up with a solution for my predicament. Her response when I asked was not what I expected, "I have an idea, but it will break your heart." I started to panic and didn't want to hear anymore, but Aglaia continued. She reminded me jobs in Patras were hard to find, and thanks to Mrs. Karras, I had one waiting for me. Through her tears, Aglaia suggested, "You should take the job, and put Maria in the orphanage just until you've saved up enough money to take care of her. Since she is a baby, she will sleep safely in a crib, and I can check on her during my cleaning shifts."

"Are you out of your mind?" I cried. "How could you possibly suggest I do such a thing? I just gave my baby a name and had her baptized. Just the thought of losing her is too much to bear. There must be some something I could do to earn a living and keep Maria with me. I will die if I give Maria up."

Gently Aglaia replied, "I know my dear, but she may die if you don't. You might have to give her up for a while to save her. You and Maria have already bonded, and if you wait any longer, you will not be able to do this."

I listened to Aglaia's suggestion but refused to consider it. Over lunch in Aglaia's tiny kitchen, we played with Maria and discussed every possible solution. We continued talking late into the night until there was nothing more to say. Older and wiser, Aglaia had always had my best interests at heart, and as much as I hated the idea, she was right. Putting my baby in the orphanage looked like the only way to get on my feet and make a life for Maria and myself.

As I considered the unthinkable, a new worry arose. What if someone took Maria? Aglaia eased my fears a bit when she told me about a declaration, a legal paper I could file at the mayor's office in the City Hall. More like a letter, this declaration would establish legal proof I was Maria's mother and formally ask the orphanage to take over her care. It was an unusual thing to do, but she thought it might give me some peace of mind.

Still not convinced I could go through with this, I agreed to accompany Aglaia to the City Hall the next morning and visit Mrs. Karras at her factory. Lying in bed with Maria, I had no plans to sleep that night. I prayed to Saint Nicholas, the patron saint of children, for the wisdom and strength to make the right decision. The rest of the night, I held Maria in my arms as I wished Mama Zoe could be holding me now – for dear life. As I talked and sang to her, I memorized every precious inch from her head to her toes. Listening to her coo and breathe were the most beautiful sounds I had ever heard.

ORPHANAGE

I HAD HOPED THE NIGHT BEFORE WAS A BAD DREAM, BUT reality hit me when Aglaia said, "You know this is the only way for you and Maria to be together. Finish your bread, and we can take the bus to the mayor's office. We will make sure you get Maria back." Riding through the Patras streets, I was heartbroken over the turn my life had once again taken. Was there no end to my misfortune? We arrived at the City Hall, where I gave Maria to Aglaia and entered. Directed to a small office where a bored-looking man sat behind a wooden desk, I asked where to file a declaration to put my child in the orphanage. He nodded toward the chair opposite him, and I took a seat. When he showed me the form, I explained I couldn't read or write, which only added to my shame. He was kind and told me not to worry. He would take notes while I talked and then rewrite them in a legal style for the declaration:

I am Hariklea Voukelatos, daughter of Efstathios, and
I live in Patras. I wish to declare this: To Mr. Mayor of Patras:

I have the honor to tell you I have acquired a ten-day-old female child out of wedlock. I happened to be without protection and paralyzed in my right leg. Poor, without any means, and ill, I cannot protect the child. Therefore, I request you to act as you see fit, and I enter this child into the Patras Orphanage for its protection; otherwise, the newborn child will die. With all respect, the person filing this request is illiterate.

Hariklea Voukelatos

It took the clerk just a few minutes to complete the declaration. I paid the processing fee of three drachmas (about 1 cent), took my copy and headed out the door for our next meeting.

Holding Maria, the three of us took the half-hour bus ride to the furniture factory where Mrs. Karras greeted us warmly. The factory looked like it employed about 50 people, all working at strange-looking machines. Each machine performed a task vital to the creation of a table, chair, or bookcase. The building resonated with the whirring of lathes, the whine of saws and the buzzing sound of sanders blowing sawdust everywhere. Mrs. Karras gave us a brief tour of the factory and explained what the job entailed.

"The job is five days a week and requires keeping the floor free of sawdust, cleaning the bathrooms, dusting the machines, and emptying the trash. Why don't you think about it and get back to me?"

The job was mine if I wanted it, so now I had a big decision to make. Looking around, I wondered how I could take Mrs. Karras up on her offer. A factory was no place for a baby. I needed someone to care for my child, but I couldn't afford to pay because I didn't have a job. If Mama was here, she could have watched Maria while I was at work. Trapped in a whirlpool of misery, the orphanage looked like my only solution.

Over lunch, Aglaia and I reviewed the day's events. I had my declaration in hand and a job offer I had to accept. Aglaia reassured me she would watch over Maria during her cleaning shifts. I had never been to the orphanage, so I asked Aglaia how she planned to leave Maria. She explained the orphanage had a safe and anonymous "Baby Receiver" mounted onto the wrought iron door out front. It was a clever wooden box that opened on two sides, one to the street and the other inside the building. Aglaia was going to place Maria inside the box, use the strap inside to secure her, ring the doorbell, and slip away into the night. A nurse inside would hear the bell or her cries and retrieve her. Then Maria's name, the date, what she was wearing, and the time she was found would be recorded in a ledger they kept in the director's office. Aglaia emphasized they were protective of the relics left with the babies: icons, notes, charms, and clothing. They saved everything. This news was of some comfort to me, so I decided to leave a note with Maria. I was her mother, and I wanted them to know her stay would be temporary. With Aglaia's help, we composed the following:

> *I have the honor to ask you to take my little girl, and maybe God will make me worthy to take her back later because right now I am merely worthy of pity and am very unfortunate. I have baptized her with the name Maria.*
> *Hariklea Voukelatos   Patras, 13 May 1953*

Aglaia took the note and placed it with the declaration on the kitchen table. When the time came, she would leave both papers with Maria in the receiver. The moonless night of May 13th, 1953, provided a perfect cover to execute our plan. It was a Wednesday, and people would be home preparing for the next work day. No one would be out on the streets. Maria had to be left secretly because the orphanage would not accept a child handed over by a parent. If someone saw Aglaia leaving the child, questions would follow, and Maria would be refused entry.

I was still not sure I could go through with it when Aglaia approached me carrying, Maria late that evening. She was dressed in a white jumper and swaddled in a warm blanket. Holding Maria one last time, I kissed her and whispered, "My love, may God keep you safe in his arms until I can return for you." Loosening my grip on my precious Maria was the hardest thing I had ever done. As Aglaia slipped out of the house, I fell to the floor in anguish. How had my life come to this? Lying there sobbing, I didn't feel the cold stone floor beneath me. I was in as dark a place as I had ever been.

When Aglaia returned, I was still on the floor. She took me in her arms, helped me to a chair and reported, "Everything went smoothly with baby Maria. I gave her a kiss for you, said a prayer, and strapped her in the box along with the papers. No one saw me come or go." I was thankful Aglaia's mission had been successful, but it did little to ease my worries. It was soul-crushing to have Maria so near, yet so far away. We sat up talking late into the night about how to get Maria back. I had one goal now, take the job at Mrs. Karras' factory and save up enough money to take care of Maria.

WITH TIME RUNNING OUT

WITH MARIA SAFELY DELIVERED TO THE ORPHANAGE, IT wasn't long before our lives settled into a quiet rhythm. We were grateful for the companionship and Aglaia appreciated the extra rent money. Each morning we ate breakfast together and went our separate ways. Aglaia walked to the orphanage or the hospital depending on her shift, and I took the bus to the furniture factory. Mrs. Karras' job was a Godsend. It didn't pay much, but I was treated well and didn't mind the work.

Every afternoon when I got off the bus, I took a detour home so I could walk by the orphanage. Now a permanent fixture in my life, it was an unfriendly looking structure. Made of concrete, three-stories-high and surrounded by a ten-foot wall, it looked like a prison. Windows covered with iron bars and trees like witches' brooms added to the compound's forbidding appearance. It certainly didn't look like a refuge for children, but it was home to my Maria, so each day I sat on the curb near an open window hoping to hear sounds of her. One time

I was sure I heard Maria's voice, and it gave me hope for the day I could retrieve her. In the meantime, it felt good to be near her.

On days when Aglaia worked in the orphanage, I hung on every word of her "Maria" updates. Any news about her was a gift, but it was demoralizing to miss seeing her reach growth milestones: Maria was crawling, her hair had grown in natural curls, and she was talking now. I couldn't help but wonder what her first word was or if anybody even heard it.

The months flew by, and before I knew it, 1954 had arrived. Greece's involvement in WWII and a Civil War took a heavy toll on the tiny country. Poverty, disease, and hunger were widespread, even in the places that cared for children. Aglaia shared her growing concern over the shortage of food, beds, medicine, and nurses at the orphanage. She feared the children were not being cared for properly. Older children were sleeping three or four to a bed. Maria was small for her age, so she still slept in a crib, but those days were coming to an end. There was very little solid food left, and as one year turned into two, many orphans were showing signs of malnutrition and neglect. I was still no closer to retrieving Maria and worried she would not survive there, let alone thrive.

I was living on the hope I could get her back, so Aglaia's news that dreary day in March 1956, hit me like a thunderbolt. "Rather than let their poorest children die, Greece is opening its orphanages to foreign adoptions."

I couldn't believe it was true. Greece would never let its children go. Family, not money or possessions, is what mattered to Greeks.

"Who's getting these children?" I cried.

"The United States has many couples eager to adopt. Orphans could start leaving as early as May."

I was worried and terrified about what could happen to Maria. They couldn't send her away; she was *my* baby. The note Aglaia wrote and left with Maria said I would come back for her. *What about the paper I filed at City Hall? Did both of those mean nothing?* I was frightened. Surely there must be something I could do. Aglaia tried to ease my despair by adding, "The selections have not been made yet. You still have a little time."

"Time, time for what? I am going to the orphanage tomorrow after work to find out what's going on. Will you go with me?"

"Maria is my Goddaughter. Of course, I will come."

I spent the next workday in a daze, going through the motions and thinking about my upcoming visit to the orphanage. When I got home from work, Aglaia was waiting for me. I gave her a quick nod and headed straight to the bedroom to change my clothes. Standing in the doorway, she revealed she had called the orphanage earlier in the day and scheduled an appointment with the director himself, Mr. Londos. Wearing the only decent dress I owned, I headed out the door for the most important meeting of my life. While we walked, Aglaia told me two things: It was remarkable Mr. Londos was taking time out of his busy schedule to listen to me, and he was not happy the mother of an orphan had shown up. She advised me to remain calm, hold my head high, and tell him my story.

Director Londos' office was messy and more substantial than I expected but furnished with a desk, chairs, tables and a small cabinet. On the wall hung the familiar icon of Saint Nicholas. I had prayed to him for strength and wisdom many times in my short life and hoped he was listening now. Aglaia pointed to a table covered with large books, each with a year written on the cover. Those were the ledgers where the nurses recorded the vital information and noted items left with the babies in the receiver. Somewhere in that pile was Maria's ledger and the papers left with her on May 13th, 1953.

On the director's desk, I saw stacks and stacks of paper files. They covered every inch of available table space, and each one had a name written on it. It looked like the selection process had begun. I wondered about the children those files represented. *What would become of them? Who would be selected to live in America? Who would not?* I was shocked the fate of so many young lives rested in the hands of just one man.

Mr. Londos was slim and tall for a Greek. Unhappy about the meeting, he did not smile as he introduced himself to me. "I understand you have a child in this orphanage," he declared.

I held my head up, answered "yes," and asked if I could tell him my story. He nodded, folded his hands on the desk, and listened as I began. I started at the beginning in Nikolis and told him about the circumstances that led me to leave Maria in the baby receiver three years earlier.

When I finished, Mr. Londos agreed I had suffered tremendously, but he was not sympathetic to my situation. He explained Aglaia had told me the truth about the orphanages.

All of them were overflowing with desperate children. Conditions in every place that cared for orphans were deplorable. Something had to be done to save the youngsters, even if it meant giving them up. The United States and Greece had worked together and passed Refugee Relief legislation to facilitate the adoptions. His final words shook me to my core: "Most adoptive parents will want babies or toddlers. Your daughter is almost three, and this is her opportunity to have a better life. She should not miss out on such a great chance."

"But she is *my* daughter. You can't just send her off to another country and let strangers raise her."

He acknowledged my love for Maria but reminded me nothing had changed. I still couldn't care for my child, and this was the best option. Hot tears streamed down my face and formed a wet circle on my dress as I realized the meeting was not going well. When I told him the declaration, I had signed at City Hall was to prevent something like this from happening, he shared a truth I was not prepared to hear. "Filing that document proved maternity, but it also gave me, as the orphanage director, sole guardianship of Maria. I, not you, will determine what happens to her. And I say Maria would be better off growing up in America."

The final blow came when Mr. Londos scolded me for using the orphanage for free childcare. He reminded me this was a place for orphans, not for children with parents. If he had found me, he would have given Maria back. He added, "You can't show up here after three years and take her back. There are rules to follow and laws to obey. If you can reimburse the orphanage for three years of room and board, then you can take her, but I doubt you have that kind of money.

"You're right, Mr. Londos; I don't have that kind of money. But from the papers left with Maria, you knew my name the night she was left. Why didn't you search for me?"

"I am sorry I have no answer to your question. It was an oversight. We should have followed up." Then he shook his head and muttered something about turmoil, too many children and too little help.

"Please, sir, isn't there some other way?"

"No, I'm afraid not. I am trying to do the right thing for all these children. For Maria's sake, she is going to America. My decision is final."

I sat there nearly out of my mind, unwilling to believe what was happening. "I took precautions to avoid this very thing. You can't do this to me," I wailed. Mr. Londos waited a few moments and then made a futile attempt to comfort me.

"The terrible things you have experienced don't need to define your life or Maria's. At 19, you are still a teenager with your whole life ahead of you. Someday you would meet a man, fall in love, and want to have a child with him. The adoption you fear is in your and Maria's best interest; you should go on with your life."

With that, Mr. Londos stood up and said, "I'm sorry this meeting is over."

I had done everything possible to protect and keep Maria since I had arrived in Patras. Now in an instant, my dream of reuniting with her was over. Strangers in another land would raise her, and I would never see her again. Blinded by tears of rage and pain, I stumbled out of the office in disbelief. I had lost my beautiful child and didn't see how I could go on. With Aglaia's help, I managed to make my way home. I fell into bed and sobbed into my pillow the tears of a heart broken into a million pieces. A knife to my gut would have hurt less. I had lost everything that meant anything to me; I prayed for death and couldn't see how I was going to survive.

I spent the next few days in a fog of denial about what happened. I kept hoping the meeting with Mr. Londos was a bad dream, or he would change his mind. Sadly, neither were the case, but that didn't stop my fantasy of running into the orphanage, snatching Maria out of her crib and make a run for it. When I couldn't do it, I hated myself for being such a coward and directed my anger inwards. Feeling ashamed, hopeless, and depressed, I tortured myself with questions of self-doubt. *Had I done the right thing? Will her adoptive parents love her as I would have done? Will Maria ever look for me, or would she hate me for abandoning her?* My days were long and tearful, but the nights went on forever. Even slumber was a fickle friend. Sleeping brought me sweet dreams of Maria but waking revealed the cruel truth. Maria was gone forever.

Still raw with grief, I forced myself to go back to work the next week. I was miserable, but I didn't want to lose my job. Sweeping floors inches thick with sawdust, dusting machinery, and scrubbing bathrooms was independent work, so I was able to hide my despair. The loud, whirring machines afforded me privacy as they concealed my sobs while the floor, covered in sawdust, absorbed my tears, leaving only wet dimples behind. When I got off the bus after work, I no longer took a detour by the orphanage to sit on the curb and listen for Maria. I never wanted to see the place again, so I took a different route home.

It was months before I was able to work an entire day without falling apart at least once. I slowly made my peace with what had happened and went on with my life. I would never forget, but I refused to be defined by my circumstances. Maria was in America now, a fact I had grudgingly accepted. I could only hope she had a family who loved her and treated her well. Maria was my child, and I would always love her, but now I had a different dream for us. I clung to hope that when Maria was older, she would look for me and we would meet again someday. It gave me another reason to live.

One day while eating lunch alone, Vasilis Konstandis sat across the table from me. A lathe operator, I had noticed him around the place the past four years, but we had not spoken. Short, with dark, brooding features, Vasilis had a warm, relaxed manner that made him popular with the other workers. I was still uncomfortable around men, so I let him do all the talking and ate in silence. He showed up at lunch the next day and the next. Warm and funny, he gradually got me to talk, and a seed of friendship grew. Over the next several years, our friendship became something more. It took me a long time to trust a man again, but Vasilis was patient and understanding. He knew I had endured a terrible ordeal but did not pry and push me for answers. Nine years later came a marriage proposal. We exchanged vows at the small church behind Saint Andrew's Cathedral on Saturday and returned to work on Monday.

Soon I was pregnant with Baby Katina. I worked long as I could until the baby arrived but knew my working days had come to an end. I gave notice and thanked Mrs. Karras for helping me when I needed it the most. Meeting her in the hospital changed my life in a way I could never have imagined. She gave me a job when work was scarce and treated me with respect and care. Mrs. Karras made it possible for me to leave the darkest, most desperate place I had ever known and find happiness with a husband and family.

For the first time in a long time, I was happy. Staying at home with my baby was a luxury I thought I'd never know. With an adorable daughter and a husband who loved me, I had a family of my own and a life I thought I'd never see. Living with Vasilis and Katina was comfortable and predictable. Katina was my world, but sometimes late at night while she was sleeping, my thoughts turned to Maria. *Where was she? Was Maria loved and happy? She was still my daughter, and I missed her every day.*

Ten short years later, Vasilis was diagnosed with diabetes. My heart was broken again when he died from kidney failure caused by the disease. A young widow with a ten-year-old child to care for, I needed to find work. Job prospects for a woman like me were limited. There weren't many times in my life I felt lucky, but getting a job cleaning the public bathrooms was nearly perfect for me. It came with medical benefits and a lifetime pension. The work wasn't easy, but it provided me with a secure financial future, something I never had before.

ELLEN'S STORY

LIFE ON VISTA DRIVE

IT WAS AN UNUSUALLY RAINY DAY IN SAN DIEGO, BUT THE
dry earth needed the rainwater so badly, Alyce and I didn't mind. Sitting
at Alyce's Formica-topped table sipping coffee and scanning the *San
Diego Tribune*, we were Ellen and Alyce, just two friends solving the
world's problems. I was about to set the paper aside when I saw a heading: "Greek Adoptions." Intrigued, I read further. It was March 1954,
and the report described the dire conditions in Greece's orphanages
where too many children lived in dreadful circumstances. Greek insti-
tutions didn't have enough room, food, or nurses to care for them, so,
in a gesture of compassion, Greece was allowing foreigners to adopt its
poorest citizens. The article went on to say a Greek American organization had already formed a Refugee Relief Committee to handle the
U.S.-bound adoptions from Greece.

I mentioned the article to Alyce, who asked if adoption was something Richard and I had ever considered since I was having a hard time getting pregnant.

"We have discussed adoption a few times, but never pursued it because I didn't want to give up trying. Last month we learned our dream of having children is unrealistic; Richard is sterile. Here we had been trying to have a baby for years, only to find out he could never give me a child. What a shock! All this time, I thought the problem was me." That fact did little to ease the hurt though. *Real* women got pregnant and had their own babies, they didn't adopt another woman's child, and *real* men got their wives pregnant and carried on the family bloodline. This new reality left us both heartsick, but it did not deflate our starry-eyed dreams of having a family.

For Richard and me, two young lovers from the Grand Canyon State, life looked a lot like a John Wayne movie set of red hills and endless desert horizons. In the late 1800s, Bisbee was a hardscrabble mining town on Arizona's raw frontier. Names like Brewery Gulch, Tombstone Canyon, and OK Street conjured up images of bar brawls and shootouts on the roads where men were as rough and hard as the rock they mined. The discovery of a rich vein of copper underneath Bisbee changed the town overnight. That copper also changed the lives of anyone willing to crawl underground and pry it from the earth with nothing more than a shovel, sweat, and a strong back. Word spread quickly mining jobs were there for the asking, so people from all over the world made their way to Bisbee.

I was born Ellen Johnson in Bisbee's Copper Queen Hospital just as WWI came to an end. My parents had immigrated from Sweden (father) and Finland (mother) five years earlier. Once they learned of employment available on the frontiers of Arizona, they traveled the long miles to Bisbee to work in the mines. We did not have much money, but I grew up in a loving home with parents who adored me and nurtured my academic and musical talents in every possible way. Raised by such loving parents, I was taught to be selfless and kind-hearted. To my friends, I was "Sweet Ellen," who could always be counted on to share, to keep a secret, or to help with a chore. Occasionally, I was taken advantage of, but it did not stop me from embracing life with generosity and trust.

In stark contrast to my childhood, Richard Pace was born in Austin, the heart of Texas, and his family moved to Bisbee when he was three-years-old. His father became a prominent lawyer who drank too much and was home too little. His mother abused him verbally and beat him daily for a long list of insignificant infractions like having dust on his shoes or uncombed hair. Whip-smart and athletically gifted, academics and sports helped him to survive his turbulent childhood. However, his parents' destructive child-rearing left Richard ill-equipped for life as a husband and father.

Richard and I met in high school at the weekly YMCA dance. We were a storybook picture of two kids falling in love from different sides of the tracks. He was from Tombstone Canyon up north where the bankers and lawyers lived, and I lived down south in Lowell with the miners and the cowboys. I was just as tiny and petite as Richard was tall and lean. Romance bloomed, and the miner's daughter married the lawyer's son in December of 1940. We made our home in Upper Lowell, just a stone's throw from my old neighborhood.

Richard worked underground as a copper miner for the Phelps Dodge Mining Company while I worked above ground in the company offices and the mercantile department. After our first year together as a married couple, world events tore us apart. The U.S. entered WWII, and Richard joined the Navy. It was incredibly hard to say goodbye to him at the bus station and to return to my life living alone, hoping he would return safely.

Richard's stint in the Navy became his ticket out of Bisbee, with his first inkling of love for the ocean and a view of life beyond his small mining town. He completed his Basic Training in San Diego and was stationed at Pearl Harbor during the war while I spent long months alone in Bisbee. Exactly three years, three months, and three days after Richard entered the service, he returned to Bisbee. He was home just long enough to pack us up and move back to San Diego where we rented a small house in El Cajon. We spent the next few years working to build the "1950s American Dream" of a home, a car, and hopefully a few kids in the yard. I paid the bills with my job at a mortgage company while Richard completed his education on the GI Bill. Shortly after graduation, he landed his first job, teaching U.S. History at nearby City College. With two salaries, we built a new home in nearby La Mesa and moved ahead with our plans to start a family. We could not have guessed we would never have children of our own.

I kept the paper from that day in Alyce's kitchen and studied the rest of the article on Greek orphans. The Greek American group handling the U.S. applications was called the American Hellenic Educational Progressive Association or the AHEPA for short. Interested couples had to be recommended by an AHEPA member to receive one. Once they had the letter, they could contact the AHEPA's central office to see if they qualified to adopt a Greek child. I had never seriously considered adoption, let alone choosing a foreign child. Maybe this idea was worth considering. Richard and I even knew a Greek couple who might be able to help us. Louis and Voula Poulos had been close friends of ours for years. They owned Athena's, a Greek restaurant we frequented. I wondered if they knew about the AHEPA. With nothing to lose, it was a place to start.

Driving home, the despair I had felt since Richard's diagnosis gave way to a glimmer of hope. Thank goodness I'd read the newspaper today.

Maybe that article was the answer to our prayers. I hoped Richard wasn't expecting a home-cooked meal tonight because we were going out for Greek food. As the day crawled by, I busied myself with housework and errands while I watched the clock for Richard's return from work. He had barely set foot inside the door when I announced, "Hi honey, I hope you're hungry because we're going to Athena's for dinner." In the car I told Richard about the newspaper article and to my relief, he was interested in finding out more about the AHEPA. Adoption was our last hope to become parents, so we prayed God would show us if there was a child for us.

The pungent smells of lamb and oregano emanating from Athena's affected us before we even reached the front door. The place was full of hungry diners enjoying Voula's Greek chicken and *pastitsio*. We put our name on the list for a table and headed to the counter where we spotted our friend Louis Poulos. As I took the seat next to him, I noticed a small blue and white enameled pin on the lapel of his coat. I studied it carefully, and I saw it read AHEPA. It was difficult to hide my excitement as I asked him about his pin.

Louis smiled, "The AHEPA is a service organization initially founded to assist the early Greek immigrants who came to America. With time, its focus evolved to promoting charitable and educational activities across the U.S. for citizens of Greek descent. I have been a proud member for ten years and know very well the AHEPA is trying to ease the desperate situation in Greece. WWII and a Civil War left the country in ruins. Hunger is widespread, and the suffering is catastrophic. Humanitarian aid is on the way from several countries. The AHEPA is doing their part by facilitating the adoptions of Greece's poorest citizens to America." I wanted to learn more, so when we were seated; I asked Voula and Louis to join us.

Over dinner, Louis told us the AHEPA had formed a close relationship with an orphanage in the port city of Patras, so most of the orphans would be coming from there. As he continued, Richard and I clasped hands under the table, barely able to believe our good fortune. Before we got too invested in this idea, we needed to find out if we even qualified. With our hopes inching higher, we asked Louis if he knew the requirements for adoption. He shared the following:

Non-Greek couples needed a recommendation letter from an AHEPA member.

Couples had to be at least eighteen years older than the orphan and financially stable.

Couples must comply with their state's adoption laws.

Couples had to bear full responsibility for all adoption and transportation fees.

Voula concluded, "We know you've been trying to have a child for years and it looks like you meet all the requirements. If you want to pursue this, Louis will write the AHEPA reference letter for you, and we will help any way we can."

I didn't want to get my hopes up, but I was excited to learn we satisfied every requirement! We were the right ages, held good jobs, and were upstanding citizens of the state of California. We were also lucky enough to have Greek friends. With help from Louis and Voula, adopting a Greek child might become a reality. I was sure all the recent events were not just coincidences, but God's way of telling us to continue down this path. Maybe our luck was going to change!

SHE'S A DOLL

RICHARD AND I WERE CAUTIOUSLY OPTIMISTIC THAT bright spring day in July 1954. Thanks to our dear friends, we had an adoption application in our hands. We filled out the form and double-checked the conditions for adopting. It was starting to look like this might happen. We returned the application, along with the AHEPA sponsor's recommendation letter to Voula, who mailed it to the South Bend, Indiana, office of Leo Lamberson. He was the attorney handling the U.S.-bound adoptions from Greece; the waiting had begun.

On September 19th, 1955, Richard's birthday, an envelope arrived from Mr. Lamberson. It contained a letter informing us our application was accepted. Also included was the Orphan Pre-Selection form and photograph of Maria Voukelatos, orphan #10356, a two-year-old girl who was available if we wanted her. The page was organized in three sections, each with a different title. The first section, "Particulars of Child," had information about Maria's height, hair, and eye color. She was 2'6" tall, with black eyes and blonde hair. As I looked at the photo of the dark-haired Maria, I was curious why they listed her as having "blonde hair." I assumed it was a typo, but over the next two years, I would discover more discrepancies in that initial paperwork.

The second section, "Natural Parents," addressed the whereabouts of Maria's parents. Both the father and mother boxes were checked, "unknown."

It was the last section, "Child's Life Story," that startled me the most. Maria's life story was only two lines long and read: *It was found in the baby receiver on 13-5-53 (5-13-53 in America), about ten days old. The girl is in excellent health, and the orphanage is taking care of her room and board.* I was not expecting to find out Maria was abandoned as a baby. That explained why her parents were "unknown." My first thought was of her mother and what tragic event had caused her to give up her child. How a mother could give up her ten-day-old baby was beyond my comprehension. Hariklea's life circumstances must have been so dire she had no choice but to give me up. Now due to circumstances halfway around the world, our lives would be forever linked. The saddest day of that mother's life might result in the happiest day of mine.

When we finished reading the dossier, we turned our attention back to the small black-and-white photo stapled to it. The photo showed a sour-faced little girl with dark eyes and uncombed hair, with a cowlick over her right eye. She looked sad, angry, and scared, probably all three. I don't know what I had expected, but I found the photo a bit unsettling. Adopting a child, we had not met was scary. You never really knew what you were getting into, and I worried about taking a child with severe health or psychological issues. I shared my fears with Richard and suggested we might want to consider another child.

He barked, "She's a doll. We're not going to ask for another dossier. We are going to get her!"

Thrilled there was a child for us, I didn't put up much of an argument and told Mr. Lamberson we wanted to adopt Maria. The next document to arrive was from the Greek Court of First Instance and asked for a decision about her name. Couples who wanted to change a child's name were asked to do so through the Greek court system *before* the child arrived. Richard and I decided to keep her Greek name for a couple of reasons: Maria meant "Mary" in English, and of course, Mary was the greatest name of all. Norman Vincent Peale, a man whose philosophy on life we admired, said a girl with the name of Mary had a responsibility to live up that name. It was also a pretty name and not very common back then. We felt whoever gave this child the name Maria must have felt, despite her unfortunate entry into this world, the name would be something substantial and concrete for her to hold on. We chose Elena for the middle name because it fit with Maria so beautifully; Maria Elena just rolls off the tongue. Best of all, though, was the similarity between our names; I was Ellen Marie, the mother of Maria Elena.

After choosing her name, legal documents began to arrive every 3-4 weeks. Most of them dealt with legal issues between the two countries and had to be notarized. Other mailings, such as photos and letters, came from the orphanage and were more personal. A letter from Mr. Londos, the director of the orphanage, was like finding an oasis in the desert. It sustained us and eased our worrying. In his most recent message, he reported Maria was a thriving two-year-old with a good appetite. She ate everything we gave her and never made a fuss. We were greatly relieved to hear Maria had no food issues and mealtimes would not be a problem.

January brought unseasonable cold and rain. It also brought instructions to contact the nearest Greek Consulate in San Francisco. That required us to take two days off work for the trip. We planned to take the train up and fly back home the next day. My brother and his wife lived in the Bay Area, so they met us at the train station and drove us straight to their house for the night. The next morning, they drove us to the Consul's office, where we signed our names to a document in

Greek. The Consul explained this was our consent to each other to adopt this child. Greece wanted to ensure both parents had agreed on adopting a child. I guess they didn't want Mom bringing home a surprise for Dad. The whole procedure took no more than five minutes, which left the four of us time to enjoy a day in San Francisco. We window-shopped, rode the cable cars, and ate lunch at a restaurant overlooking the bay and Alcatraz prison. By then, it was time to head to the airport and catch a plane back to San Diego. The next day it was back to work and waiting.

123 DAYS OF ABSOLUTE SILENCE

IT HAD BEEN TWO LONG MONTHS SINCE OUR JANUARY TRIP to San Francisco, and we still hadn't heard a thing. As Richard and I went about our daily lives, we wondered what could be taking so long. Every evening after work, I ran to the mailbox, heart racing, to see if there was any news, only to be disappointed. Maybe tomorrow I told myself. Having a child was just within my grasp, but I was still terrified something could go wrong. The waiting was taking a toll on me, and I didn't think I could take another disappointment.

Part of my problem was I had too much time to think. Evenings and weekends were the hardest, so I bought a scrapbook to preserve the artifacts of this entire experience. Because I wanted it to last until Maria was an adult, I spent a little more money on my selection. Her scrapbook had a green leather cover, gold brocade ties, and thick, durable pages. I had a special drawer where I had saved every scrap of paper from personal letters and legal documents to canceled checks and postage stamps. Even the ticket stubs from the train and airplane trip to San Francisco were waiting for their spot in the scrapbook.

Organizing the book in chronological order made the most sense to me. I dedicated the entire first page to that little black-and-white photograph we received so long ago. As much as the photo had concerned me, I couldn't imagine any other child for us now. When I showed Richard the page, he smiled, took it and wrote "What a doll!" next to Maria's picture. Right then, I knew I was in for a lifetime of playful teasing. Covering the blank pages with documentation of our dream was extraordinarily therapeutic and time well spent. Many of the letters and official documents from Greece were as delicate as tissue paper. As I carefully stapled and glued, the memories returned and lifted my spirits. When the book was completed, I knew it would bring joy to Richard and me for many years. It would also be a valuable tool when I told Maria about her adoption and how she came to live with us. When Maria was an adult, I hoped it would become a treasured possession and tangible evidence of how much we wanted her.

March arrived and still no word from anyone. By this time, several more couples were trying to adopt Greek children. Voula Poulos was busy helping them with the paperwork and getting ready to travel to Patras to visit the orphanage. She wanted to check out the conditions there and see if she could speed up the process because it was taking so long. My heart went out to the new couples because I knew all too well how hard the road ahead would be. Since Richard and I were further along, I told Voula I would help the others while she was away.

Now my evenings and weekends were busy helping other couples like us. Each of them was at a different stage in the process, so I assisted them with completing forms, getting them signed and notarized, and mailing all the necessary paperwork. We were members of a unique club who all wanted the same thing – to become parents. We realized our adoptions would be easier if we supported each other. When one couple got good news, we all shared in their happiness. When another wasn't sure they could wait any longer, we rallied around them and lifted their spirits with our tales of waiting. Knowing we were in this together brought me a certain measure of comfort. When difficult times bring people together, there is often an upside - the friendships that blossom between people who remain friends for life.

By April, the waiting had become mind-numbing. This journey had undoubtedly tested our patience, but never our commitment. We would endure any obstacle if it brought us closer to our dream of becoming parents. To keep ourselves busy and sane, we got Maria's bedroom ready. We chose a "Snow White" theme and spent weekends shopping for paint, bedding, curtains, and a dresser. Richard painted the room green with white trim, and we hung "Snow White" characters on the walls. It looked charming. We also purchased a few toys, including a Gerber baby doll that cried, drank a bottle, and wet its diaper. I hoped she would become Maria's first friend.

Everything was just about ready. The only thing missing was a wardrobe for our three-year-old. I assumed Maria would arrive with only the clothes on her back and need everything. I was secretly relieved when Richard said he didn't want to go to Sears with me. Clothes shopping for my daughter was the icing on the cake, and I was going to enjoy every minute of it. I pulled into the parking lot and entered the store with a spring in my step. Was it me or did Sears look more inviting today?

Inside I headed straight for the children's department. Until now, I had avoided that area in Sears. That was where the moms shopped, and I was not one of them. When I was forced to shop there for a gift, I felt like an imposter trespassing where I didn't belong. Adopting Maria changed everything. Now I was a member of the "Mom" club. The feelings of being an interloper disappeared, and the hole in my heart filled with happiness. As I picked through the racks loaded with colorful playsuits and dresses, I watched the other mothers shopping for their children. What may have been an ordinary task for them was anything but ordinary for me. I took my time as I fingered the clothes Maria would need: silky satin dresses, soft cotton sleepers, sturdy rubber sneakers…everything. I carefully selected items for play and special occasions, knowing Maria would have plenty of both once she arrived. As I made my way to the register with my treasures, I realized this labor of love had taken most of the afternoon. There would be lots more shopping trips for Maria, but I doubted any of them would bring me the indescribable delight of this first one.

May brought Maria's birthday, so we sent her a box of clothes along with a letter. Hopefully, someone in the orphanage would translate it for Maria. To our amazement, we received a thank-you letter from Mr. Londos and another picture of her in return. Maria still looked sad and mad, but that picture became a lifeline for us. We knew our little girl was safe and coming to America; we just didn't know when.

May also brought Voula home from Greece with fantastic news for everyone. She had visited the orphanage and spent time in Patras with Mr. Tsaparis, the lawyer handling the AHEPA's adoptions in Greece. Voula told us four adoption decrees, including Maria's, had been cleared by the Greek court and another two were on track. That was the best news yet! We had just completed one of the biggest hurdles in our adoption journey. Maybe that's why we hadn't heard a word in so long; the Greek courts didn't move any faster than the American ones.

A SLIGHT DETOUR

IT WAS WASHING DISHES ON A WARM JUNE DAY AND daydreaming about Maria's arrival. Mr. Lamberson had scheduled her to fly to New York on Swiss Air and then on to San Diego with TWA. One of the largest and most trusted airlines in the country, it mattered she was in such good hands. TWA was one of the first airlines to volunteer its planes for the 1953 Refugee Relief Act. Mindful of the expense for the parents they also discounted the adoptee's airfare.

We were still waiting to hear when she'd leave Greece when a TWA agent called with news that sent me reeling. She told me Maria was in New York with Mr. Lamberson! He had traveled there to meet the plane and assist the 11 orphans with their connecting flights to cities across America. Six of the children had reached their destination; they were going to families in New York. Maria was one of five youngsters with connecting flights the next day, so she was taken to the St. Moritz Hotel and put up for the night. Directions from Mr. Lamberson about Maria's arrival in San Diego would follow soon.

For a moment, I was not sure I had heard everything correctly. Was Maria in the United States? I couldn't believe it. Not a word for four months and the first news we hear is Maria has already arrived in America! Why hadn't anyone called and told me she was leaving Greece? I wouldn't have been able to do anything, but I would have appreciated the update. I collapsed on the sofa, so overcome with relief and happiness I could not speak or even call Richard. When I finally composed myself enough to call him with the news, he was thrilled. Just one more airplane ride and Maria would be here, or so we thought.

I awoke the next day, giddy with excitement about Maria's impending arrival. Today I would receive the final phone call with information on Maria's flight with TWA. I kept myself busy recleaning the house and watching the clock. Mr. Lamberson finally called, but the news was not what I expected.

He had planned on a quick, overnight, turn-around in New York. What he had not prepared for was a child too sick to fly. He explained Maria was not in "excellent health" as stated on her adoption papers. The youngest child on the plane, she had suffered the most on the long, rough flight that originated in Athens and stopped in Geneva, Switzerland; London, UK; Gander, Canada; and finally, New York. Maria was scheduled to take a TWA flight to San Diego the following day, but the airline determined Maria was too malnourished, dehydrated, and anemic to fly. Now what?

Mr. Lamberson was not angry, but I could tell this unexpected development had thrown a wrench into his busy schedule. Maria was grounded, and he had to get her medical attention. Unable to stay in New York, Mr. Lamberson was going to drive Maria back to his home in South Bend and check her into a local hospital. When the hospital cleared her to fly, he would book Maria new tickets from Chicago to San Diego. I trusted Mr. Lamberson, but I told him I was worried about an eight-hour drive with a three-year-old. Maria was sick, and any number of things could go wrong. He did his best to allay my fears, but it was futile. I felt helpless and afraid for my little girl who had already been through so much. Mr. Lamberson promised he would call with news the next day, but I knew I'd be on pins and needles until I heard they had arrived safely. With plans in place, Mr. Lamberson shared a touching story about Maria:

"When I met the plane, I was surprised to see Maria was wearing only white sandals and an airline blanket. The nurse who traveled with the children told me Maria was too sick to keep anything down. In a gesture honoring their homeland, many children left Greece with a pouch of Greek soil pinned to their clothes. The nurse tried to save Maria's, but it was impossible. Everything she had was ruined and had to be thrown out.

While carrying her through the airport, a woman stopped me and asked why the little girl had no clothes and was wrapped in an airline blanket. I explained where Maria had come from and how sick she had been. The woman stopped and immediately opened her suitcase on the floor. She pulled out a white t-shirt, a sleeveless floral dress with a matching ruffle around the bottom, and a white sweater. Holding them up, she declared, 'Take these, she is about my daughter's size. Maybe they will fit her.'

I put Maria down, and we slipped the t-shirt and dress over her head. The clothes were a perfect fit, and she looked adorable in them. I thanked the kind woman and told her she had just given Maria her first American outfit."

What a lovely story. It lifted my spirits to know there were such good people in the world. A woman's simple act of kindness had brightened the world for a sick and frightened a little girl. It seemed Maria had a guardian angel watching over her until I could be there. In the meantime, I would stay by the phone and wait.

The next morning Mr. Lamberson called with an update and some good news. There was nothing seriously wrong with Maria. She was resting comfortably in the hospital but needed a full week of blood transfusions and nutritional supplements to get her healthy enough to fly. It was June 23rd, so he booked Maria on a TWA flight from Chicago to San Diego for July 1st, 1956. He would call us with the details about her arrival. Only one more week to go!

ELLEN'S "LIFE MAGAZINE MOMENT"

THE SLOWEST WEEK OF MY LIFE CRAWLED BY, AND FINALLY, Mr. Lamberson called with an update on Maria's health and her flight information. A week in the hospital had done her a world of good. The numerous blood transfusions and vitamins had done their job, and Maria was cleared to fly. It was the best news ever! On the morning of July 1st, Mr. Lamberson would drive Maria to Chicago, where she would catch a plane to San Diego, arriving about 3:00 p.m. He was unable to accompany her to California because he needed to return to work assisting other orphans. Once again, I was worried about my little girl traveling such a long distance alone, but my fears were put to rest by Veronica Booth, a TWA stewardess from San Diego. She volunteered to fly back to Chicago over her July 4th, weekend and escort Maria to San Diego. Another angel! I hoped I would be able to thank her in person at the airport.

The adoption of Greek orphans by San Diego couples was big news back in the 1950s. As July 1st, drew near, friends, relatives, news reporters, and photographers called to learn about Maria's arrival time. All of them wanted to meet her at the plane when she landed. Congressman Bob Wilson, who was instrumental in getting visas for the San Diego adoptees, was even going to be there.

My nerves took a beating as the big day grew nearer. One moment I was over the moon with excitement, the next I was in tears, scared something would go wrong, and Maria wasn't coming. I must have checked and rechecked Maria's bedroom 20 times to make sure it was ready. Four pairs of little shoes were lined up on the closet floor, while frilly dresses hung above. The dresser was full of play outfits and underwear, and a Gerber baby doll was waiting on her bed.

I had imagined this day a thousand times; confident it was going to be one of those beautiful *Life Magazine* moments. *Life* was the gold-standard in the 50s, and almost everyone had a weekly subscription. Every week we waited with excitement and anticipation to see the cover for the next issue. Who could forget the iconic photographs of the soldier and his girl running to each other across the rain-soaked tarmac or the sailor kissing his girl after returning home from WWII? When Maria's plane landed, flashbulbs would pop as guests and journalists strained to get photos of the little girl who had traveled so far. Maria and I will lock eyes and run to each other; then I'd sweep her up in my arms and smother her with kisses as the crowd cheers. I couldn't wait.

At long last, the big day was here, and it was time to head to the airport. Maria was in the air and would land in an hour. I was so excited I could scarcely keep my wits about me as Richard, and I changed into our best clothes. We were headed to the car when I stopped, ran back into the house, and grabbed the doll off her bed.

"I don't know if she had one in Greece, but I thought if we brought her a doll, it might make her feel less alone and scared."

"Great idea, Mom."

I hopped in the car, and we were off. Today was the day! No more delays! Nothing else could go wrong! As we drove, I glanced at other drivers headed our direction. Barely able to control my excitement, I wanted to shout, "I'm going to the airport to pick up my three-year-old daughter today, what are you doing?" To Richard's relief, I kept quiet, and we reached the airport in record time. I noticed a good-sized crowd had already gathered at the end of the terminal near the TWA gate. Friends and relatives mingled with photographers checking their cameras and journalists clicking their pens. Congressman Wilson, never one to miss a photo opportunity, was nearby pressing the flesh.

The atmosphere at the gate was festive, the air electric with excitement and curiosity. Then in an instant, the mood changed, and everyone quieted down as a TWA plane taxied toward our gate. It was the flight from Chicago! Suddenly time slowed to a crawl. It took forever to wheel the rolling stairs up to the cabin door so that the passengers could depart. As they exited, my heartbeat jumped with every person who came into view, only to return to normal when I saw it wasn't Maria.

At last, we saw a young woman holding the hand of a tiny girl as they made their way down the steps and toward the terminal. Maria was wearing the floral print dress given to her by the kind stranger at the airport and pulling the stewardess close behind. As they entered the building, the crowd moved back, and Richard and I moved forward so she could see us. The stewardess released Maria's hand as I got down on my knees, holding the doll in my outstretched hands. Photographers were poised for a great picture as I said in a measured tone, "Hello Maria, I have waited a long time to meet you."

Well, she had other plans. Maria took one look at me, screamed at the top of her lungs, and sprinted past me as fast as her little legs could carry her. Her sandals with rigid leather soles made a loud clapping sound on the tile floor as she tore past gates filled with passengers. Everyone turned to look at the little girl who had caused such a ruckus. An alert agent bolted past me and caught Maria halfway down the terminal. Kicking and wailing at the top of her lungs, he wrestled her back to the gate. It was apparent Maria wanted nothing to do with anyone, least of all me. In front of everybody, Maria threw herself down on the floor in a full-blown tantrum. Shrieking in Greek, I couldn't understand what she wanted or needed. I felt helpless as I stared in disbelief at my daughter. In an instant, my heart-warming moment had turned into a nightmare. I could see the headlines now, "Orphan Rejects Mother." My humiliation was complete. I was grateful for one thing that day, thank God *Life Magazine* was *not* here!

The photographers realized there was not going to be a photo op that day, so they packed up and left. Congressman Wilson was gracious and congratulated us as he left without a publicity photo of him with Maria. Friends wished us well and said they looked forward to meeting her at another time. A few joked it looked like we had our hands full. I couldn't disagree as I tried to figure out a way to calm Maria, get her into the car, and then home.

GETTING MARIA HOME

AS I SAT THERE WATCHING MY SCREAMING THREE-YEAR-old, I scolded myself. What on earth was I thinking? In my eagerness to become a mother, I got caught up in the romance and excitement of her arrival and had not fully considered how all of this would affect Maria. Two weeks ago, she was living in the Patras Orphanage that had been her home for more than three years. After a problematic plane trip and week in the hospital, everything she had ever known was taken away. I had failed to grasp a harsh reality: Maria was an institutionalized toddler who had been thrust into mainstream American life overnight. She had lost her mother, her motherland, and her mother tongue. No wonder she was afraid of everything and everyone.

An hour later, still in shock by Maria's behavior, Richard and I were wondering what to do next. Unless we planned to live at the airport, we had to find a way to get Maria home. Blanche, one of my oldest and closest friends, had stuck around to offer moral support. We had grown up together in Bisbee, Arizona, and moved to San Diego after the war. She had a daughter named Susie, who was five years older than Maria. As I looked at Susie and the doll in my lap, an idea born of desperation began to take shape. I knew Blanche wanted to help, but it was her daughter I hoped to recruit.

"Blanche, I'm not sure this will work, but I am out of options, so here's my idea. Would you let me borrow Susie for one night so I can get Maria home? I think she is more comfortable with children and might be more willing to go with us if Susie comes along."

Blanche laughed and agreed. "That makes a lot of sense, and it's not a bad idea. Let me talk to Susie and see if she can help you."

I had known Susie since she was born, and she would go anywhere with me. Going with Maria was another matter. Susie had seen Maria's behavior, and I hoped she wasn't afraid of her. Blanche returned shortly with Susie.

Smiling, Blanche announced, "Susie said she thinks Maria talks funny, but she wants to help you."

Maria's cries had softened to sniffles as she sat on the floor. I handed Susie the doll and asked her to give it to Maria. As she approached, Maria stopped and looked up. Susie held out the baby and motioned for Maria to take it. Warily, Maria took the toy and held it close. It warmed my heart to think she owned at least one toy in the orphanage. Susie was gentle and patient with Maria, and it didn't take long before the girls were playing together. Susie had found a way to reach out to Maria and earn her trust without saying a word.

We let them play until I thought we should try to guide Maria out of the airport. I took Susie's hand and motioned for her to take Maria's. Slowly, Maria took Susie's hand and stood up. Bit by bit, I started walking: one step, two steps, three, and we were off at a snail's pace. It was like walking with a human land mine; it could blow at any second. Only a few more steps and we were outside the terminal heading for the car. I opened the door and let Susie into the back seat first. Maria quickly followed and sat right next to her. Richard and I jumped into the front seat, locked all the doors, and took off. There would be no stopping along the way. Maria was tired and scared, and we needed to get her home.

Pulling into the driveway, we leaped out of the car in unison. Richard blocked one back door, and I blocked the other. Ready for anything, I opened the door slowly. I took Susie's hand, and she took Maria's as they got out of the car. So far so good, now all we had to do was manage the 72 steps up to the front door. I wasn't sure Maria could even walk up that many stairs. She looked dog-tired. She had most likely used up any strength she had left from the long airplane flight. Half-way up Maria couldn't walk any farther and collapsed on the stairs. Now what? Richard tried to carry her, but his imposing size and height scared her, and she wouldn't let him pick her up. Susie was still holding Maria's right hand, so I approached her at a glacial pace and took hold of her left. I waited until her hand relaxed in mine before I bent down and carried her the remaining steps to the front door.

Once inside, I headed straight to her bedroom and laid Maria, clutching her doll, on the "Snow White" bedspread. Susie climbed on the bed right next to her, and before long, both girls were sound asleep. Richard and I took advantage of the quiet and sat down for a little supper to discuss our remarkable day. Now that Maria was finally here with us, the embarrassment I felt at the airport seemed insignificant. We were already able to laugh about most of it. It was clear the little girl with the cowlick over her eye was going to bring us lots of excitement. As I walked to the bedroom to check on the girls, the house felt different. It was a subtle yet powerful feeling. Our house had become a home, and my dream of being a mother had come true.

ADJUSTMENTS

THOSE EARLY WEEKS WITH MARIA PROVED TO BE MORE challenging than we expected. The day before Maria arrived, I called Sharp Memorial Hospital to schedule a medical exam for her. I was thrilled when the hospital went above and beyond and arranged for a doctor to come to the house. A house call from a physician was a rare event, even in those days. Dr. Bishop examined Maria, ran a couple of tests and immediately put her back in the hospital for another week of blood transfusions and vitamins. This time Maria was not alone, as she had been in Indiana. Every day brought a steady stream of well-wishers, many of whom donated blood for her transfusions. My brother drove down from San Francisco to meet Maria and donate his blood. For years afterward, he liked to say, "Now with my blood in her veins, Maria is part Swedish."

During her hospital stay, I learned some troubling information. The doctor told me not only was Maria anemic and malnourished, but she had no idea how to chew food. Her entire diet in Patras had consisted of a milky liquid. She was never given any solid food to eat.

No wonder she was in such poor health! Little did I know one of my first jobs as a new mother would be to teach my daughter how to chew. I assumed the people at the orphanage had done the best they could under the circumstances. Still, I hated to think about how long any child could have survived in that place.

Home from the hospital a week later, Maria had more energy than before, but nothing like any healthy three-year-old I had ever known. She spent her days napping and playing in the backyard sandbox, which she called "sand-o-pie-o," with her doll Susie. How sweet she named her baby doll after Blanche's daughter, her first friend in America. I loved to hide in the kitchen and watch her play with Susie in the sandbox. Maria spoke to her in Greek at first, but as she learned English, so did Susie. That little doll quickly became her most cherished possession. Everything came to a standstill if Susie was missing because we knew there would be no peace until she was back in Maria's arms.

We dedicated those early days to get Maria the nutrition and the rest she so desperately needed. Cooking healthy food was easy but getting her to eat it was another matter entirely. I put the chewing lessons on hold for a bit because everything I put in front of her ended up on the dining room wall. Juice, soup, Jell-O, and baby food: all of it went flying. I quickly figured out only white-colored foods were safe from her deadly arm. I was happy to accommodate her, but I soon learned that even her white food had to be prepared in a specific way. One day I made a batch of creamy potato soup but added black pepper on top for flavor. The soup was safe, but she made me pick out every speck of pepper before she'd touch it. We kept at it, and it wasn't long before long Maria branched out to foods of other colors.

One day, an odd thought struck me: I remembered I had received a little note of acknowledgment from Mr. Londos, the Director of the Patras Orphanage. It was in response to a letter, pictures, and some gifts I had sent over for Maria. I went back to my scrapbook to find that note.

Sure enough, Mr. Londos' letter said Maria was one of the easiest eaters he had ever seen! I could only laugh. Did the man stick to a standard response to all parents who wrote? He was a great salesman, or he had never met Maria. Probably both. We would make sure Maria's menu expanded, but we had a long road ahead.

In a couple of months, Maria had learned to eat soft foods on her own and took a liking to applesauce and puddings. That's when I noticed a new troubling attitude. When she sat at the table, her head hovered just above her dish, and she wrapped her arms around her plate, guarding it like it might be pulled away at any moment. Was this what mealtime in Patras had been like for her? How awful for a three-year-old to have to fend for her food like that. I was not prepared to see this aggressive sign of self-preservation, and it left me very sad. Frankly, I was more than a little shaken when I realized such behavior might well have been necessary. It took everything I had to hold back my tears as I watched Maria eat. I hoped unconditional love and time were all she needed to trust us.

Maria had been with us for three months when we decided to take her to the Methodist church we attended. She was eating soft foods and was stronger now. For her first outing, I chose a pink dress with a black bow in the back that matched her shiny, black, patent leather shoes. I knew Maria loved the dress as I watched her twirl and spin, but she went completely crazy over the shoes. She immediately jumped and stomped around the house, yelling, "papoogie, papoogie." I looked in my Greek dictionary and learned it was the three-year-old pronunciation for "papoutsi" or "shoe." Maria loved the way the new shoes looked, but she loved the noise they made on the wooden floor, even more, giggling at all the new sounds she could make.

Inside the church, we took seats in the back of the sanctuary where we could make a quick exit if necessary. We managed to keep her quiet but were relieved when the service was over. At the social hour that followed, everyone made a big fuss over Maria. They wanted to hold her, pinch her cheeks, and talk to her. I tried to keep a straight face as friends raised their voices in the hope more volume would turn English into Greek. Poor Maria didn't understand a word they said, and it wasn't long before she became overwhelmed by it all and began to cry. The attention of all the well-meaning strangers was too much for her, so we took her home. Maria hadn't been around that many people since she had landed at the airport. Back home, I undressed her, found Susie, and put them to bed. Maria promptly fell asleep.

A couple of hours later, I was preparing dinner when an ear-splitting scream stopped me in my tracks. I ran to Maria's room to find her standing atop a pile of her new shoes and dresses. Looking in the closet, I saw it was empty, save for the coat hangers. The dress I had hung up after attending church was on the pile along with her beloved black shoes. What prompted this behavior? I bent over and picked up a shoe, but she screamed, grabbed it back, and threw it on the pile. Her reaction when I tried to hang a dress back in the closet was the same. She was trying to communicate something was wrong, but I didn't know what.

I finally connected the dots when Maria went to the closet and slammed the door shut. Like her food, Maria was afraid her shoes and dresses would be taken away. She couldn't see them if they were behind a door. Her tantrum was like a stab in the heart as I realized what I had innocently done. How horrible my little girl had to scream to keep something of her own. It took me a few deep breaths to realize this behavior would be less challenging to remedy than the food issues had been. I lined her shoes up along the wall and hung her dresses on hangers *outside* the closet. It made for a busy looking bedroom, but Maria was happy.

The battles over Maria's shoes seemed never-ending. She owned a pair of blue tennis shoes which she called her "blue shoes," but she still used Greek to describe her black patent leather shoes as "papoogies."

Maria was madly in love with those shoes. Every time we got ready to leave the house, even for the nearby grocery store, she wanted to put her "papoogies" on, and we had a screaming scene! She refused to leave the house without them, so Richard or I had to carry her and her tennis shoes down the 72 steps to the garage. Once we got Maria in the car, she calmed down, and I could put on her "blue shoes." We knew the "shoe scenes" wouldn't last forever, but both of us looked forward to the day when her obsession with those "papoogies" was over.

Relaxing on my bed after Maria's latest "papoogie tantrum," I opened my dresser and removed the white sandals she was wearing when I met her. Those little sandals were the only possession that survived the flight from Greece to America. Made of leather, they were not stylish in any way, but rugged, sturdy, and built to last. The white toe-strap, scalloped on both edges had tiny holes strategically placed to form a wavy geometric design, and the ankle strap with its small metal buckle and clasp was still in perfect condition. Both soles were stiff as boards and had been repaired at least once with leather patches nailed to the bottom. It was apparent she had spent many hours in them. What amazed me was how anyone could walk in them much less run. Maria must have "clomped" everywhere she went.

Whenever I looked at them, the same desire came to mind. How I wished those shoes could talk, I had tons of questions to ask them. They were on Maria's feet in the orphanage and when she left Greece for the long plane ride to New York. They went on the road trip to Indiana, where she spent a week in the hospital. And finally, they were on Maria's feet when she walked into the San Diego airport to meet us. Those shoes represented the bridge between her Greek past and her American future. They supported my little girl at a time when she had nothing and carried her to a place of hope, health, and love. Both her shoes and her scrapbook would be gifts for Maria on her 21st birthday.

As Maria was learning English, a funny thing happened. We had learned a few Greek words to better communicate with her. However, it wasn't long before she began to replace a Greek word with her English version. This behavior nearly set our communication skills back to square one. For example, when Maria first arrived, we never had any bathroom "accidents." When she said, "gee-a-mo," it meant she wanted to go to the bathroom. Now she was trying to use English, and the word sounded like "broom." So, until we figured it out, there were quite a few pairs of wet pants.

Four months had passed, and as I watched Maria play on a warm October day, I barely recognized her from the little girl we first met. The changes she had undergone were nothing short of miraculous. It seemed like only yesterday I was scrubbing down the dining room wall after one of her first meals. Maria was still a picky eater, but she was eating solid foods now and had gained some weight. She no longer protected her food with her arms while she ate, and her shoes and dresses were inside the closet. Her vocabulary had grown by leaps and bounds. I wouldn't be surprised if she spoke only English by Christmas.

Looking back, despite everything we had been through, adopting Maria was a marvelous experience for us, and we wouldn't have missed for the world. We had loved her from afar for more than a year, but we were head over heels in love with the real thing. Now we were the parents of a spunky little girl who was full of life and not afraid to yell her mind. We were in for the adventure of our lives!

The original Patras orphanage was built in the late 1800's housing Greek children for over 100 years. The statues resting on the cornice and the iron gate are all that were saved from the original building.

The doctor is opening a Baby Receiver at the Athens orphanage.
The orphanage in Patras had a similar one mounted on the front gate.

The new orphanage was opened on the same site in 1972. The statues in the courtyard and iron doors are from the original building. The Baby Receiver is gone, and a decorative pram and doorbell are in its place.

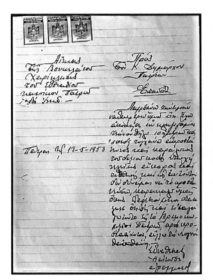

The document on the left is the written version of Hariklea's oral declaration at the City Hall. Aglaia wrote the note on the right for Hariklea. Both were left in the Baby Receiver with Maria.

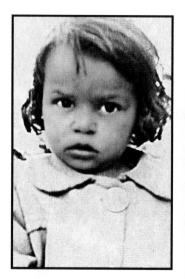

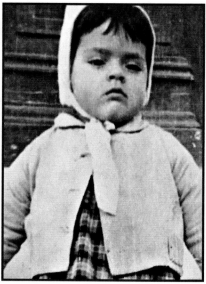

These are the first pictures Ellen and Richard Pace received of Maria.
They were taken in the orphanage.

Richard and Ellen Pace in their 30's; before Maria.

Maria arrived in New York on a Swiss Air DC-9 after stops in Zurich, Geneva, London, and Gander, Canada. There were 17 adults, 11 adoptees, and one live dog on board.

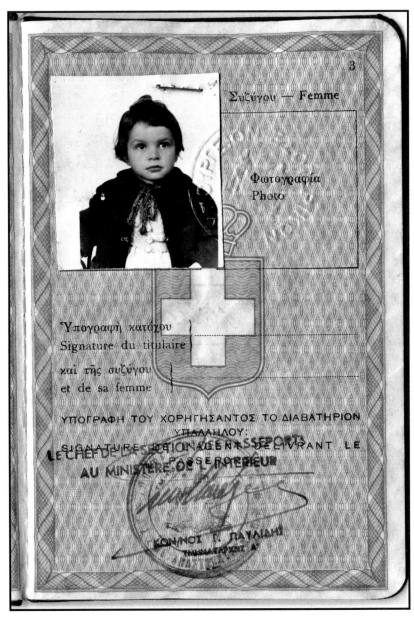

Maria's 1956 Greek passport

Four adoptees arrived in New York in late June 1956. Flights to their new homes would be aboard TWA. This photo was featured in *Skyliner*, TWA's company magazine. Maria is on the far right.

Taken at the party for the San Diego Greek adoptees and their parents, Leo Lamberson is sitting in the middle with Maria on his lap. Congressman Bob Wilson is on the left.

Brother Michael arrived from the Athens orphanage in 1958.
He was five years old when he joined the Pace family.

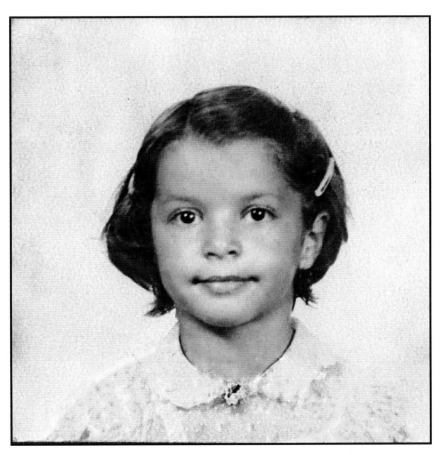

On November 7, 1962, Maria became a U.S. citizen.
This photo appears on her Naturalization Certificate.

In 1984, Hariklea Voukelatos and Maria reunited after 30 years.

Hariklea is with her daughters, Katina is on the right and Maria on the left.

MARIA'S STORY

A NEW NORMAL

I WAS THREE WHEN I ARRIVED AT MY NEW HOME ON JULY 1st, 1956. I have no memory of the flight, my week in a South Bend, Indiana, hospital, or my dramatic arrival at the airport. In hindsight, maybe that was a good thing. My first memories as Maria Pace are of a party thrown for the San Diego parents and their newly adopted children. From the photographs I have seen, it was a festive affair with nine couples and 11 adoptees in attendance. Even Leo Lamberson, who mediated the AHEPA adoptions, and Congressman Bob Wilson, who secured the entry visas were there. The photos of beaming parents posing with their precious children do not depict the uniqueness of the evening: with the Greek children unable to communicate with their parents and vice versa, there must have been two separate parties; the Greeks in one group and the parents in another.

Flying beds and children like me are the lasting memories I have of that evening. It was my first exposure to Greek kids since I had arrived, and it was comforting speaking my native language again. Banding together, we explored the sizeable house, peeking in every cupboard and closet we could reach. When we discovered the house had an elevator, there was no stopping us as we rode up and down for hours. Heading upstairs, I peeked in a bedroom where I saw beds that looked like hovering spaceships, ready to take off and fly right out of the room. I was astonished. Each bed was a homemade wooden box that held a twin-size mattress and hung from four ropes attached to the ceiling. Even with a footstool, they looked impossible to get in and out of without falling on your head. To this day, I've never seen such unusual beds.

It didn't take long to settle into my new life with the Paces. During the week, there were errands with Mom, naps, and playdates with the neighbor boy. On weekends there were excursions to the beach, parks, and the zoo. The beach was my favorite. The salty air, waves pounding on the sand and birds squawking overhead transported me to another world. I spent hours playing in the sand and running from the waves as they tickled my toes. The highlight of any beach day was bodysurfing with Dad. He'd put me on his back, and I'd hold on tight while he swam into deeper water. It felt like flying as he jumped into the perfect wave and, with our chins up and bodies stiff, we rocketed toward the shore. Poor Mom, who never learned to swim, watched us from the safety of her towel on the sand.

The San Diego Zoo was another favorite destination. I liked the big cats and the bears, but I couldn't get enough of the monkey and elephant habitats. Maybe I liked the way the elephant trunks and monkey tails curled around things. I don't know, but on one of our visits I got them confused and yelled at the top of my lungs, "You elephants better get down from those trees before you hurt yourselves!" Mom and Dad must have been so proud!

Not long after I arrived, I taught Dad a valuable lesson: The idea of children and the reality of raising them were two very different things. Dad built our house himself and always had a project in the works. His latest job was to finish the concrete patio in the backyard. The area was large, so he sectioned it off into large squares with wooden frames to make pouring the cement easier and keep the patio level. One day, while Dad was at work and Mom, was busy with the laundry, I stood at the back door admiring the newly built frames. I could not resist. I snuck outside and invented a game of hopping from one frame onto the other until I had landed on each one. No one knew what I had done until Dad poured the cement that weekend. It was a mess. Nothing was level, and the water drained right towards the house! Dad figured it out quickly. I don't remember if he got angry with me, but his reality changed that day. Life before me: everything was just how he left it. Life with me: count on everything below four feet to have been monkeyed with.

I have nostalgic memories of those early days with Dad and Mom, and I'm thankful for the good times we shared. What weighs heavy on my heart as I write this is how few I can recall. The following year my parents were introduced to a local woman pregnant with twins who wanted to give them up to a suitable home. Mom and Dad took me along on the interview as a living testimonial that they were acceptable parents. They passed muster because Richard Jr. and Deirdre joined the Pace household a week after they were born, making me a big sister at the age of four.

I vaguely remember the trip to Mercy Hospital to pick up the twins. We were waiting in the lobby when a nurse came out holding two babies. Swaddled in white blankets, one bundle wore a blue hat and one a pink hat. There were smiles all around as visitors and staff members fussed over the babies while Mom and Dad signed some final papers. Mercifully both were asleep, so Dad drove while Mom and I each held a baby. For a while, I thought when you wanted a baby, you just drove to a hospital and bought one, or two.

Back home, the twins slept soundly in their cribs in the next bedroom. I liked the idea of being a big sister, but it took time and effort to get used to my new role. Those two babies created a lot of work for everyone in the house. It seemed like the crying, eating, and diapering never stopped. I helped as best I could, but there was only so much a four-year-old could do. There were still outings, only not as often and rarely with both parents. Those babies ended my days as the center of attention. My time as an only child had lasted less than two years. Little did I know there was another momentous change in store for me.

When the first phase of the Refugee Relief Act ended, there were still a few orphans left in Greece. My parents were contacted and asked if they could take a boy from the Athens Orphanage. With two girls and one boy already they agreed, and five-year-old Michael arrived in 1958 making us a family of six. Only five months younger than me, he was small and shy with black hair, green eyes, and arc-shaped scars that ran the length of each leg. While in Greece, Michael had suffered from rickets, a children's disease that caused his leg bones to become soft and bow outward due to a lack of Vitamin D and calcium in his diet. Fortunately, the surgery which involved breaking and resetting his leg bones was successful. So successful, in fact, years later Michael ran the quarter mile for his high school track team!

As it did for me, a better diet in America made a dramatic difference in Michael's health. Unlike me, my new brother knew how to chew solid food when he arrived. I was glad I didn't have to teach Michael how to eat, but Mom made me spend 30 minutes each day giving him English lessons. I resented that job. I spoke English now and had better things to do with my time, but Michael was bright and in no time at all was fluent in English.

It didn't take long to realize how determined Michael was. By the time he was seven-years-old, he knew he wanted to work in medicine. He never wavered from that early decision and went on to become an operating room nurse by his 30s. A gifted musician, Michael could play any woodwind instrument he picked up. As time passed, having a brother so close in age was a gift. We became each other's confidante and best friend. To this day, Michael is my hero.

With two adults and four adopted children, my family was now a world-class genetic stew. Dad was basketball-player tall with black hair and blue eyes. Mom, a Scandinavian beauty, was barely 5'2" with sparkling green eyes and porcelain skin. The only similarity the twins shared was their slim build and height. You would not guess Richard Jr., with his blond hair, brown eyes and turned up nose, was related to his twin sister Deirdre, with dark hair and eyes and a prominent nose. Even the Greek kids didn't look alike. Except for our short stature, I had brown hair and eyes while Michael had curly black hair and green eyes.

Most Friday nights, we ate dinner at Mom and Dad's favorite Mexican restaurant. The six of us must have made quite an impression because people often stopped by the table, gave us a quizzical look, and asked, "All yours?" I loved watching their expressions when my parents answered, "Why yes, they are!" It was the 1950s, and people didn't know what to make of such a diverse looking family, so they gave a puzzled nod and moved on. Mind reading would have been a fun skill to have as I watched the wheels turning in their heads with questions.

Mom had an ingenious way of handling questions from strangers about her children's looks. On outings with Mom, someone usually asked if I was her daughter. When she replied yes, the usual response was, "Oh, she must look like her father." Mom always smiled, nodded, and never took any offense. Later she would look at me and say, "There's another left-handed compliment." It wasn't until I was an adult; I understood how genuinely gracious she had been.

The absence of a genetic connection to my California family never really bothered me. As a small child, I was always aware I was different… I was Greek… I spoke Greek… I was adopted. When I was older and lost my native language, being Greek was still part of my identity. It wasn't bad; it wasn't good. It just was my normal.

Like Mom and Dad, I dealt with my share of unique situations. I had no baby pictures to fawn over like my friends, and it was impossible for me to relate to people who fretted over inheriting Grandpa Jack's big nose or Aunt Edna's curly hair. If they shared concerns about diseases that ran in their families, I commiserated and tried not to worry about every single one for myself. When I had to draw a family tree for a science class, my assignment was to learn how I could *not* be related to my siblings: wrong eye color, wrong hair color, wrong blood type – a genetic impossibility. Even dating in high school created some unexpected drama. Hanging out with brother Michael, we had to convince more than one jealous boyfriend or girlfriend we were siblings. Was the absence of a genetic link a curse or a gift? I am still not sure.

Like many orphans, I indulged in "adoption fantasies" to fill in the blank spots about the circumstances of my birth. Most of mine were about my birth mother and depending on the day, the contrast in what I daydreamed ran from A to Z. One day she was a poor, homeless, beggar living on the streets. The next she was Maria Callas, the mistress of Aristotle Onassis who bore him a love child he could not acknowledge. That explained my love for singing, but not my lack of an operatic voice. I even had a funny birthmark between two toes I was ready to show Mr. Onassis should he come calling. Poor Mom spent two years trying to scrub that birthmark away.

When I turned six, I learned life as a teacher's kid had its benefits. It got me accepted into the Campus Lab School (CLS), an independent elementary school on the San Diego State College campus. The school was innovative and sought-after to the degree that parents had to register their children the day they were born. I didn't register until I arrived in San Diego at age three. It was right after WWII, and the school's unwritten affirmative action program included admitting Jewish and International children, and now a Greek girl. Also, Dad knew a couple of professors with a daughter my age who was already accepted. They recommended it to Mom and Dad and were instrumental in getting me admitted.

As part of the School of Education, CLS served students who wanted to become teachers. Twice a week, between 20 and 30 prospective educators sat in the back of our classroom and watched master teachers instruct us. It was a win-win situation. The college students experienced teaching in a real setting without leaving campus, and we had the entire college at our disposal. We swam in the Olympic-size pool for PE, learned silk screening in the Art Department, and studied Astronomy in the planetarium; the perks went on and on. Spending six years with the same group of kids was another gift, which resulted in life-long friendships. It would be years later when I had my classroom; I fully appreciated the million-dollar education I had received.

A third-grade assignment sparked my desire to see Greece. Mrs. Bacon had assigned each student a report about a country of their choosing. Not surprisingly, I chose Greece, so I could learn about where I was born. I researched its history, geography, cultural customs, and food. Everything I read about Greece fascinated me and fueled my desire to see the place. With the report finished, my final task was to design the cover. I spent hours drawing the Parthenon on Greek blue construction paper until it was third-grade perfect. I can still recall how proud I felt when I handed my report to Mrs. Bacon. I received an "A," but by now, it was not the grade that turned my desire to visit Greece into a dream.

Third grade was memorable for another notable event; it was the year I became a U.S. citizen. The day's importance was lost on me, but I knew it was special because I got to miss school and I wasn't even sick. Plus, Mom and Dad wore their church clothes, and I got a new dress. We drove to downtown San Diego and entered the courthouse. It was a massive and uninviting place, so I stayed close to my parents. We headed for the courtroom but didn't get very far before I was whisked away for a photo, and Mom and Dad were asked to sign more papers.

We *heard* the courtroom before we found it. The scene inside was chaotic, with adults and children dressed in odd clothes, shouting in strange languages. A judge walked in, quieted the group, and spoke for a long time. He concluded his remarks by leading everyone in the Pledge of Allegiance and passing out our Naturalization Certificates. With shouts of glee and congratulations all around, we exited the courtroom and enjoyed a reception of cookies, coffee, and punch.

During those formative years, I fell in love with gymnastics. Small for my age and still physically weak, our family doctor told my parents to enroll me in a sport to build up my body strength. I had seen a gymnastics exhibition by a local club and wanted to give it a try. I took to it instantly and found I had a natural aptitude for the sport. Between workouts six days a week, exhibitions, and meets, gymnastics was my life. One week my team was performing during an NFL half-time show, and the next we were competing against the best gymnasts in the state. When my competitive days were over, I worked as a coach and found my calling. I wanted to work with children. I found tremendous joy in helping kids conquer their fears to learn difficult stunts while making them feel safe, valued, and included.

GROWING UP A-PACE

I FINISHED THE THIRD GRADE AND HEADED TO THE fourth, with a better sense of my identity. However, life at home became more difficult as Dad's behavior started to change in a troubling way. I was only nine years old and knew something wasn't right, but I didn't know why. Dad was rarely relaxed and always seemed on edge. Evenings in the back yard playing catch or tossing horseshoes gradually stopped as he became emotionally unpredictable. Date nights with Mom tapered off and eventually stopped. His easy laugh was replaced with angry outbursts that became more frequent. Slowly, before my eyes, the fun-loving dad who took me body surfing and taught me how to ride a bike changed into a tortured adult.

As Dad's mother had done to him, he started to hit us for minor, kid-like infractions, such as getting our clothes dirty, leaving our rooms messy, or using incorrect table manners. Most times, Dad used a belt, but there were times when he chose more harmful tools of discipline. The beatings were bad enough but making us go to our rooms and wait for him to administer our punishment was just plain sadistic. Those were the times I fantasized about my birth father.

Being a teacher's kid had its drawbacks too. Teacher hours meant Dad got home from work around 3:00 p.m., the same time we did. Why couldn't he have a job like other dads and work until 5:00 p.m.? I felt cheated out of two hours of peace every day. That equaled 10 hours a week, 40 hours a month, and God only knows how many hours a year. It added up, and I resented it all.

Supporting a family of six meant financial strains, so Dad taught summer school in July to make ends meet. With Dad at work, we could relax and play without fear of inadvertently committing some infraction that resulted in punishment. One day we'd play Stone School and Jacks, games played by Mom when she was a girl. The next, I was a fierce cowgirl who climbed trees and shot cap guns better than my brothers.

Kingdom was my favorite game. As the oldest, I appointed myself the queen, who lived in a splendid castle and ruled over her vast backyard kingdom. I made my brocaded robe out of old dining-room curtains and transformed a patio chair into my royal throne. I commanded Michael and Richard Jr. to do my royal bidding and sent them to the dungeon, made from old pieces of wood if they refused to obey me. We let our imaginations run wild in a world where anything was possible. The problem was, no matter how much fun we were having, the clock was ticking. Dad would be home soon, and my kingdom would come crashing down.

August was Dad's time off. Most summers, we stayed home because Dad had home projects he wanted to complete. One summer, we took a vacation to Arizona, Mom, and Dad's old stomping grounds. Our first stop was Phoenix to visit Aunt Elma, Dad's sister. She was the highlight of the trip. Two years older than Dad, six feet tall, and cheeky, she was a fearless big sister and not afraid to speak her mind. I watched in awe as Elma bossed Dad around like a little kid. If he got irritated, she diffused his anger with sass and humor. Even more incredible was seeing such submissive behavior from the most powerful man we knew. I thought she was the coolest big sister I'd ever met, and I wanted to take her home with us. I did take with me some of the techniques and the wit she used to deflect people's anger and frustration. Thank you, Aunt Elma – those tactics come in handy to this very day.

We left Phoenix and headed south to Bisbee, Mom and Dad's childhood hometown. For years we heard stories about the hardscrabble mining town with names like Brewery Gulch, Tombstone Canyon, and OK Street. I looked forward to seeing those places for myself. Copper was no longer king in Bisbee, but the civic leaders had wisely preserved much of the city's nineteenth-century charm. Mom and Dad took turns being tour guides as they showed us around town. We traveled one mile underground on a copper-mine tour and strolled up Brewery Gulch to OK Street, where Dad had delivered newspapers as a boy. I thought the street name was odd but laughed out loud when Dad explained its origin. Part of the street was home to the red-light district, which the men in town thought was "OK," and the name stuck. We peeked in the windows of the schools they had attended, loitered outside their childhood homes, and sat on the steps of the church where they married in 1940. In Tombstone Canyon, we posed for pictures underneath the Pace Avenue sign, named after Dad's grandfather, Dempsey Calhoun Pace, a prominent civic leader. Seeing the Pace name on a street sign was cool.

After a long day of sightseeing, Dad and Mom took us to dinner at the Copper Queen restaurant, Bisbee's finest. Sadly, even on vacation, Dad struggled to control his temper. Surrounded by other people, he could not be overtly abusive, so he became passive aggressive and covertly cruel instead. At dinner, Dad got angry for no reason we could see, put his fork down, and announced he was too upset to eat. Our meals had been served, so we were forced to eat in front of him or ignore our food and go hungry. By then our stomachs were in knots, and even if we'd wanted to, we couldn't eat. I was confused: I hated him; I was terrified of him; I loved him.

Life with Dad was not easy for Mom either. Most destructive of all was how he shattered her dreams of having babies and the social life that came with academia. He never hit her, but easily intimidated her with his size and disposition. When Dad started teaching, he did not embrace college life. Work was work, and he wanted no part of socializing with his colleagues. It would have meant the world to Mom to attend even one faculty tea or party, but it was not to be. The closest she got to college life was typing up Dad's exams. For such an outgoing, warm person, the seclusion must have been heartbreaking. If she was angry, frustrated, or hurt, she never showed it while we were around. Mom paid a heavy price for the family she wanted. Resigned to her lot, she gave up her dreams and turned her energy to taking care of her family as best she could, including caring for Dad.

Mom told me when they'd tried to start a family without success; Dad had blamed her. He wanted a family, and adoption was their only chance for a child, so he *reluctantly* went along with the idea. That revelation, which came to me later in life, sure explained a lot about why things happened the way they did. They adopted four children, but I wondered if the truth lay in Dad's inability to bear the loss of a "biological dream child." *Was each of us a reminder of Dad's failure as a man and the end of the Pace bloodline? Had we rescued my parents from childlessness only to remind Dad of his infertility?* I didn't have the answer, but Dad's resentment and anger grew with each year.

As time passed, we struggled as a family unit. The twins, Richard Jr., and Deirdre had an unexpected and overwhelming impact on all of us. They just seemed to be wired differently. From an early age, both displayed hyperactive, angry, and highly addictive personalities. Brushes with the law and expulsions began in elementary school. I didn't even know you could be expelled from grade school. Sadly, Mom was forced to drive to two schools each morning and afternoon.

For me, the middle-school years brought the common fears and insecurities associated with early teenage life. Music became a lifeline that helped me through those awkward years. I had taken violin and piano lessons but discovered singing gave me the most joy. I was lucky enough to have a choir teacher who fostered that love, and I enjoy singing in choirs to this day.

I got good grades with one exception. No matter how hard I worked or stayed after school to seek extra help, I barely passed my math classes. Every semester, my report card would show all A's and one D, always a D in math. I could almost feel a wall go up in my brain, sealing off any hope of comprehension. It was awful and embarrassing. I jokingly blamed my difficulty on the "New Math" curriculum introduced in elementary schools in the 1960s. Not surprisingly, none of my teachers bought that excuse.

For Richard Jr. and Deirdre, life became worse the older they got. Drugs ended their school days with neither finishing high school. By their late teens, they were full-blown drug addicts living on the streets. Breaking into houses and stealing financed their drug habits. Not even our own home was spared from their thievery. It was a gut-wrenching blow for Mom and Dad to arrive home to a house that had been ransacked and robbed by their daughter. A long stint in the local jail stopped Richard Jr's criminal ways, but Deirdre's troubles with the law escalated. The climax came with an FBI chase and a ten-year prison sentence for bank robbery. My parents were used to watching FBI agents on their television screen, not standing on their doorstep looking for their child.

When I look back on all four Pace children, it's hard to believe we grew up in the same household. There were the "big" kids and the "little" kids, and each group was treated entirely differently. Michael and

I excelled in school, music, and sports, yet we suffered the most from Dad's violent behavior. We thought if we were perfect, Dad would love us more and treat us better. It was hard not to feel resentful when, even though we tried to do everything right, we were his targets, and the twins sucked the life out of our parents without repercussions. Thank God we had each other as a lifeline of support. When we could manage it, we found a quiet place to sit and talk. Dad's most recent outburst, the latest humiliation in front of the neighbors, the twins latest brush with the law, or the pros and cons of our latest runaway plan were frequent topics. Those stolen moments helped us survive life in the Pace household.

While Michael and I spent our days in fear of doing something to provoke Dad, Richard Jr. and Dierdre were fearless. They did whatever they pleased and were never held accountable for their behavior. Deirdre was the worst. She did and said anything she wanted. Her go-to retort when she got in trouble was, "You're not my real parents, I don't have to listen to you." I was horrified she would say something so cruel, but dumbstruck when Dad and Mom let it pass. Ill-prepared to handle two drug-addicted teenagers, my parents suffered in silence with their pain. It was an awful day when I realized my parents were afraid of Richard Jr. and Deirdre. What kind of hell must it be to fear your own children? I wondered if, in their darkest moments, Mom and Dad regretted adopting the twins. I know there were times when I did.

High school was full of contradictions. Intent on making the most of those four years, I dove in head-first. I was a good student, a three-sport athlete, and a cheerleader, all while I sang alto in the school choir. All my activities provided an excuse to spend hours outside the house. At school and in my extracurricular activities, I felt safe and appreciated. I also felt isolated and phony. Afraid others would learn the truth about my home life; I became a master at avoidance and excuses. I always had a reason why meetings or gatherings couldn't be held at my house.

Even those 72 steps leading to the front door helped keep my secrets. When friends picked me up, no one complained when I asked them to honk their horn and wait for me on the street. When I was dropped off, those same steps gave me time to steel myself for what was waiting on the other side of the front door. I envied my friends' parents who had large social circles and got together often. Mom and Dad were invited but never accepted any invitations. We never had guests come to the house for a meal, let alone to stay over.

My trouble with math continued in high school, but this time an "F" jeopardized my eligibility to participate in sports and remain a cheerleader. My math teacher, Mrs. Drake, met with school officials to decide how to handle the situation. She was permitted to change my grade to a D- on the condition I repeated the class next year. Receiving a second chance because my teachers thought I was a "good kid" had a significant impact on me. I did not have to suffer the humiliation that could have ruined my high school years. Educators like Mrs. Drake, who understood you don't throw out a student's success to punish failure, still hold a special place in my heart. Their compassion affected my approach to teaching children who struggled with academics, especially math.

For reasons I never understood, Dad's abuse of Michael increased when he started high school. Teachers and coaches questioned him about the bruises and cuts, but Michael always had an explanation. Back then, children were not protected by teachers, so no one stepped forward on his behalf. With no one to help him, Michael left home and lived most of his high school years at a friend's house. That dear family opened their home, fed him, and gave him a safe place to stay; they saved his life.

I never really acknowledged the impact my fractured family life had on my social development. I learned to keep everyone at arm's length and protect myself from the judgment I was sure would follow if anyone knew about my home. A few years ago, while visiting with a friend from elementary school, she shared, "When you joined our class in the first grade, I liked you immediately. We got along great, and I wanted to be your best friend. Over the next few years, I tried and tried to get close to you, but I couldn't, and I never understood why." Her revelation shocked me. At such a tender age, had I figured out it was safer to fly under the radar and keep outsiders at arm's length? I wasn't even aware I had done such a thing. It saddened me to think I may have treated other friends in the same way.

After high school, I pursued an Education degree at San Diego State. Mom and Dad would not or could not help me with college expenses, but they let me live at home if I was a full-time student. To pay for school, I taught gymnastics at the local Recreation Center and waited tables at a coffee shop near campus. By then the Campus Lab School had closed, and our entire elementary school became part of the School of Education. It was strange attending college classes in the same rooms where I was a child. Thank God the desks were bigger.

With two jobs and college classes, I still made time for friends, including the man who would become my husband. Shortly after graduation, I married and moved to Vancouver, WA, where he worked as a Fire Marshal, and I began my teaching career.

THE DARK IN THE MIDDLE
OF THE TUNNEL

AS A YOUNG ADULT, DAD'S CRUEL COMMENTS HURT ME more than any beating. One month before my 20th birthday, we had a terrible argument. I don't remember what we fought about, but the conversation ended when Dad yelled, "You'd be in some gutter if we hadn't adopted you." I could take it no more. I turned around, walked away, and moved into an apartment the next week. I knew Dad felt terrible about his hurtful comment to me, but there are some things you *never* say to an adopted child. He gave up his entire weekend to help me move, but he never apologized. Yes, his comment cut me to the bone, but I also knew it did not define his whole being.

Time passed, and we reconciled. He walked me down the aisle on my wedding day. Still, the hurt exceeded my capacity to forgive him completely. It tainted my thoughts about adopting a child because I feared even thinking the words, he had said to me. One day while discussing Dad's behavior with Mom, she said something as shocking as it was true: "Considering your Dad's side of the family, I think adoption was a good thing. You were able to dodge the genetic bullet of mental illness." By "mental illness," I assumed Mom meant the generational abuse and crippling depression that ran in the Pace family. In Dad's case, infertility was a blessing. The Pace bloodline would end with him.

When Dad turned 57 years old, he faced the battle of his life, cancer. Facing his mortality changed him into the kind of husband and father he should have been. He spent his last ten years hugging us often and saying "I love you" every time we saw him. We enjoyed eating out, walks around the lake, and just sitting on the porch. Those are my favorite memories of Dad. To this day, I do not understand why he could not or would not apologize for the pain he caused. It would have meant more than anything to me.

As I write this, I have considered another truth; Dad did not possess the capacity to love another person unconditionally. He was raised by brutal parents, who likely were raised by parents just like them. Dad was ill-equipped to be a loving husband and father because he had not experienced love himself. He became what he hated most, and brutality in the Pace household continued through my generation. Unable to give of himself, Dad provided us with "things," and if he did not get the payback he wanted, he lashed out violently.

Three days before my 30th, birthday, Mom called and told me Dad had died. I knew his cancer had returned with a vengeance, and it was only a matter of time. I was not completely surprised by her call, but I was not expecting to hear he shot himself in the backyard with a 12-gauge shotgun. They were watching TV the night before when Dad excused himself to use the bathroom. Mom heard a door slam and figured Dad had gone outside for some fresh air. When he didn't return, she went looking for him. It didn't take long for her flashlight beam to land on his slipper alerting her to what he had done.

As disturbing as that night was, it left me with an unforgettable memory of how selfless and unique Mom was. When she realized what

Dad had done, she went inside and called the police. With emergency vehicles and sirens on the way, her first concern was for the neighborhood children who would surely come over to see what happened. Mom grabbed her coat and ran up and down both sides of the street, notifying parents and asking them to keep their children inside. "Sweet Ellen" had once again thought of others before herself.

I understood Dad's decision to end his suffering, but the way he carried it out was thoughtless and self-serving. Mom did not deserve to go through such a gruesome ordeal. When I asked if he had left a note, she said yes. It contained two words; "I'm sorry." Hearing that gave me pause. Dad had never apologized for anything in his entire life. Why start now? Was he genuinely sorry, or was he protecting Mom from being suspected of murder? I want to think he was doing both. A suicide message was the first thing the police looked for when they arrived, and Dad's note cleared Mom of suspicion. I have also pondered another reason behind that "I'm sorry" which was so out of character. Was Dad's belated apology to Michael and me an apology he would never actually have to speak. Again, I'd like to think so.

I sobbed for three hours over Dad's death. I cried for the little boy ignored by his dad and terrorized by his mom, the young father playing in the surf with his little girl, and the father he tried to be his last ten years. My anger has eased, but the scars are deep, and I have not shed one tear since.

Did I win the adoption lottery with the Paces? I didn't win the big prize in the father department, but I still got a good deal. Fortune was on my side and would be even more so in my future endeavors.

ELLEN'S GIFT

THE MOVE TO WASHINGTON STATE IN FEBRUARY 1981 WAS not easy for this southern California girl. My husband's new job started during one of the rainiest winters in decades. They say the Arctic Tribes have 100 names for snow. Now living on the border with Oregon, I quickly learned a thousand new words for precipitation. The weather and location weren't the only changing factors in my life. I would be single again as my brief marriage ended in an amicable divorce.

I moved into an apartment with a girlfriend where I worked as a substitute teacher by day and waitress by night. Newly single and working jobs with flexible schedules, I knew if I was going to Greece, this was an excellent time to start planning. Once my teaching career began, I would be spending parts of each summer taking education classes, and opportunities for travel would become more limited. I started researching organized trips and tours because I thought it was a smart way to familiarize myself with the country.

As luck would have it, a friend gave me a brochure about a three-week travel program in Greece called the Ionian Village. Run by the

Greek Orthodox Church, it provided opportunities for Greeks living in North and South America to visit Greece and learn about orthodoxy at a more affordable cost. The Ionian Village was a large compound located in southern Greece that served as home base for the program. As I studied the itinerary for the adult session, I noticed the schedule included several stops in my birthplace, the coastal city of Patras. Thinking an extraordinary experience it would be to wander the streets where I was born, I wrote a check and signed up. I had the choice of two return dates: immediately or five weeks after I.V. ended. I wasn't sure what to expect, so I bought a ticket with a return date five weeks out. I would be spending over a month alone in Greece and was anxious about such an extended stay, but my intuition told me I would need the extra time.

As my departure date neared, I made a checklist of things to do. First, I began Greek language lessons from a friend to learn a few basic phrases. Losing my ability to speak Greek weighed heavily on me now, but I looked forward to relearning my first language. Next, was rereading the adoption scrapbook Mom gave me on my 21st birthday. A Pace family tradition, I can still recall the evening she handed me her treasured possession and said, "I have waited your whole life to give this to you. Here is the story of how you became our daughter." Unable to speak, I hugged her tight and hoped she could feel my love and gratitude flow into her.

Before that birthday, I had only seen the book for short periods and under strict supervision before it was secreted away in my parents' bedroom. They weren't trying to keep it hidden. The book was falling apart from old age, and Mom wanted to protect it. The green leather cover, once bound with a fancy gold brocade tie, was now held together with strips of scotch tape. Many of the pages were barely attached to the spine, some not at all. Staples, once shiny and new, were now rusted with age and stained the corners of the artifacts they held together.

The amount of documentation Mom saved was astounding. Everything was there, from the first letter of inquiry to the AHEPA about adopting a Greek child to souvenirs from my U.S. citizenship ceremony in the third grade. I found a comfortable chair, poured a glass of wine, and reread my favorite book cover to cover.

My "Orphan Pre-Selection Form" was the first legal document in the book and one of the most interesting. Typed on thin, onion-skin paper, it was packed with information. Per the checked boxes, I was 2'6" tall with blonde hair and black eyes. Blonde hair? I was illegitimate and found in the baby receiver on 13-5-53 when I was approximately ten days old. If I was "approximately" ten days old when found, could my birthday be May 2nd or May 4th? I celebrate on May 3rd, but a speck of doubt has always lingered in the back of my mind.

Letters and legal forms required by Greece and the U.S. made up most of the book. One of the most anticipated documents for Mom and Dad was a telegram from Congressman Bob Wilson. Congress had granted the visas needed to enter the U.S.!

Most new parents send out birth announcements. Mom didn't want to miss out on any "new mom" traditions, so she crafted an adoption announcement using wordplay to compare a thoroughbred race-horse and a three-year-old girl. She even assigned me a stall number and a racing handicap. Printed on white card stock and embossed in black ink, her announcement card was clever and creative.

One of the sweetest items in the book was the expense report detailing how much money Mom and Dad spent to adopt me. The cost of everything: phone calls, postage stamps, train and airplane tickets, taxicab fares, and legal fees totaled $1162.26. Mom and Dad's combined salaries totaled $8,619, so I wasn't a bargain back in 1956. It was a substantial outlay of money, but I think their investment paid off.

Cards and photos were next. What fun it was reading people's wishes for us from so long ago! There were small personal photographs of me after I arrived and professional photos taken at the San Diego party for adoptees and their parents. Near the rear of the book was Mom's journal where she compared "waiting for my arrival" to that of an expectant father. A gifted writer, she filled those pages with her love and hopes for me. To this day, I cannot read it without tearing up. Souvenirs from my U.S. Citizenship ceremony in third grade concluded the book. She had saved the small American flag, the U.S. citizenship pamphlet, and even a patriotically themed napkin.

Returning the book to the shelf, I removed the adoption decree. It contained the orphanage address, a physical link to Greece, and I was taking it with me. I didn't expect to find much, but I could not deny my curiosity about the orphanage. Even if the address turned out to be a vacant lot, it was still a tangible connection to Patras where I spent the first years of my life.

Mom saw the bigger picture in leaving this heirloom for me. She was secure enough in her parenting, not to see adoption as a threat to her womanhood. She also created a priceless historical record of a time in the 1950s when two countries cooperated to save desperate orphaned children. Years later, as I re-acquainted myself with other Greek orphans and began to write this story, I came to appreciate the incredible gift my mother made for me. Many of the adoptees I have met have little or no paperwork because their parents destroyed it. It was the 50s, and not everyone was comfortable with adoption. Some children didn't find out they were adopted until their parents died. Now many are hoping to find some answers, but they have no paperwork to guide their search. This book, with her love packed on every page, was Ellen's legacy to me.

A RETURN FLIGHT TO GREECE

IT WAS SUMMER 1984, AND I WAS ON MY WAY TO GREECE. The first leg was a five-hour flight from Portland, Oregon to New York's Kennedy Airport. New York: the big apple, bright lights, big city, and big airport. It must have been a mile to the Olympic Airlines terminal for my final connection. I breathed a sigh of relief when I saw a priest taking attendance and getting our group ready to board the plane. Settled in my seat, it wasn't until the jet lifted off the tarmac, the reality of my trip truly hit me. I was on my first intercontinental flight since I had arrived in America 27 years before.

The plane was packed with loud Greek families and an even louder Italian soccer team. Everyone on board had a cigarette and was puffing away like a smokestack. As the cabin filled with noxious fumes, I worried about surviving the flight without permanent lung damage. Fortunately, dinner was served right away so the flight crew could get everyone fed and settled in for the night. Sitting in the dark, I took a few moments to reflect on recent events. I believed things happened when the time was right. Dad's death the previous year made this trip easier for me. I didn't know if he would have been as supportive as Mom was about me returning to Greece. Being single was another blessing. It would have been difficult to take off for two months while married.

As thrilled as I was about this journey, I had to be honest with myself. Was this trip about soaking up Greek life, or did I have a hidden agenda? On a conscious level, finding a birth parent was not the reason for the journey. My motivation was to find the orphanage or at least where it once stood. Even if all I found was a vacant lot, it was an answer and would mean a great deal to me. Still, I could not deny a distinct feeling of "longing" for Greece. Something was waiting for me there.

We flew all night and landed in Athens the following morning. After spending 9 hours in a metal tube, the intense Greek sun nearly blinded us as we stumbled to the terminal. Inside, two priests greeted us, helped with customs, and directed us to our bus. The drive from Athens to the Ionian Village or (I.V.) was more than four hours, including the regular stops for food and bathroom breaks. Fortunately, our transportation for the next three weeks was a new, air-conditioned Mercedes bus. Our driver was a gregarious young Greek named Andonis, who spoke English fluently. Our guides were two American priests: Father George Savvas and Father Tom Tsagalakis. They were young, Greek, and recent graduates from the seminary in Boston. Father George was married and waiting for his first parish assignment in the fall. Father Tom was single and deferring his ordination until after he was married. Greek priests who want to marry must do so *before* they are ordained.

The long drive provided travelers with some downtime and a chance to get to know our fellow travelers. The group numbered about 40 men and women, between 18 and 35 years old, from all over the U.S. and Canada. At 30, I was one of the older folks. I worried traveling with such a large group would be overwhelming, but my worries were short-lived. Once we were on the road, people introduced themselves and shared a little about the places they called home. With a heavy dose of regional stereotyping, friendly teasing followed each introduction. Travelers from the southern U.S. took the brunt of the jokes, but no one was spared. I recall someone asking them if they could survive three weeks without eating grits or catfish. Being the sole traveler from the Northwest, I was teased about spotted owls and owning a plaid flannel swimsuit. I think the good-natured ribbing helped everyone relax and a sense of warm camaraderie quickly developed.

As we traveled south from Athens on the National Road, (Greece's only major highway), I was surprised how much Greece resembled parts of Southern California. With its arid landscape of shrubs, rocky outcrops, and anemic-looking pines, only the olive trees looked like they were thriving. The lush green leaves offered a stark contrast against the dry, rocky hills. Farther west and south into the Peloponnese, the scenery changed to orchards laden with oranges and lemons and vineyard-covered hillsides.

Leaving the National Road, we traveled on the more typical two-lane roads. It was along those roads we first saw small shrines called *kandilakia*. I had never seen anything like them. Father George explained they were built either as a remembrance for the victim of a fatal traffic accident or by the survivors of a potentially tragic accident to thank a saint publicly. Made of concrete, stone, metal or wood, they often took the shape of a little church and held Orthodox Christian icons, in addition to oil lamps. They were everywhere, and each one was unique. Word was almost everyone in Greece had one along a road somewhere. Driving through the small towns and villages, I noticed each one had a central square with a proud church at its center. Religion and family were the centers of Greek life.

Arriving at the Ionian Village (I.V.), we were given our room assignments and had a few hours to unpack and relax. I was lucky enough to be assigned one of the sugar cube cottages that slept, two people. My roommate was Georgia, a tall, slight woman from South Carolina who handled the southern teasing with grace. Her drawl and infectious laugh were endearing, and we became fast friends.

Early that evening, everyone met for dinner, a tour, and an orientation about the next three weeks. Built with Aristotle Onassis Foundation dollars, the I.V. was more impressive than I expected. There were dorms, a full kitchen with a covered eating area, cottages, an amphitheater, and a chapel, all surrounded by lush lawns and gardens bursting with tropical flowers. For the sports enthusiast, there was soccer, tennis, swimming, and volleyball. In typical Greek fashion, everything was painted white. The sea was just a short walk from the grounds and quickly became our "unofficial" private beach.

Our stay at I.V. was short. On the third day, we were on the road to our first stop. The sightseeing excursions were divided into geographic areas separated by a few days back at the I.V. Our first destination was the island of Zakynthos for one day and night. We boarded our bus and drove north to the docks in Kyllini, where we boarded the ferry and traveled west from the mainland. Much like the ferries back home on Washington's Puget Sound, they transported people, cars, and trucks to and from the islands. I walked to the top deck to feel the wind on my face and to avoid the motion sickness that had vexed me all my life. Nearby, brightly painted boats with names like Athena and Poseidon bobbed like corks in the choppy sea as their owners fished for the day's catch.

Our large group must have resembled an invading army as we disembarked on the quay of Zakynthos. Father George told us the rest of the day was ours to spend as we liked, but to be back at 7:00 p.m. for dinner. Some people hit the beaches; others visited shops and restaurants. Always up for an adventure, I joined three girls from Canada who rented mopeds for the day. Fun and easy to drive; they were the perfect way to see the beauty of this island.

As we zipped along the narrow roads, I could not believe the splendor of Zakynthos. I had seen postcards and photos, but they did not prepare me for what I saw that day. Water ranging from aqua to cobalt lapped the white sand on every beach. Scruffy-looking sheep grazed among the beehives dotting the hillsides. Greek Yiayas (grand-mothers), dressed in simple black dresses and scarves, herded goats in the hot sun while olive farmers tended their trees. Nearly every house we saw was painted white, but there was still room for an individual style. The front doors were every size and shape and painted every color imaginable. Thick wooden shutters hung on most of the windows. While some remained in their natural state, others were painted to match the bright colored doors. Geraniums of every color burst from planter boxes under the windows.

Back on the waterfront, we enjoyed a traditional Greek dinner of chicken, fish, salad, and bread at a taverna. It was a beautiful evening as people shared stories about their excursions, the people they met, or the treasures they bought. That night was also the first time many of us experienced Retsina, a drink that innocently resembles white wine. I say "experienced" because it is made with pine pitch and has a taste one does not easily forget. I thought it tasted like turpentine, but to my amazement, a few folks liked it. Laughter and Retsina offered the perfect combination to end our first day on the road. Everyone was tired and ready for bed as we boarded the bus and headed to the hotel. It had been a long day and tomorrow we would return to the mainland and make the two-hour drive to Patras.

PATRAS SURPRISE

THE FOLLOWING MORNING, WE WERE UP EARLY FOR A continental breakfast. We boarded the bus and rode the ferry back to the mainland. Heading north along the coast, Father George announced our first stop in Patras was a tour of St. Andrew's Cathedral, the largest church in Greece. Named after Andrew, the brother of Peter and one of the Twelve Apostles, the cathedral dominated the eastern edge of the city. With 12 small domes, three on each corner, and one large central dome, it was the largest, oldest and most ornate church I had ever seen. Before we proceeded, the priest leading the tour checked to see we were appropriately dressed. Women cannot enter churches wearing shorts, and both men *and* women must have their shoulders covered.

The cathedral tour led by the parish priest was more exciting and ghoulish than I expected. Learning Saint Andrew was crucified in Patras when he was 80 years old was a surprise. Feeling unworthy of being killed like Christ, his cross was X shaped, and he was bound upside down rather than nailed. Parts of Saint Andrew's cross, a small finger, and the top part of his skull were kept as relics and revered in the church. They attract a steady stream of pious visitors. The priest explained this phenomenon of worshiping relics is common practice in many European churches. I found it to be rather macabre and wondered where the rest of his body parts were.

After the tour, we drove west into the heart of Patras. Ever since morning, I had kept close to Father George and made sure I sat near him on the bus. I pulled out my adoption decree, handed them to him and whispered, "Father, I was adopted from a Patras orphanage in the 1950s. Here is a copy of my Adoption Decree. It is in Greek, and I cannot read it. Would you mind having a look and sharing anything interesting you find?" Father George glanced at the papers and offered to look at them over lunch.

Stepping off the bus and onto the quay, I could see Patras was no small city. Stretching for miles along the coast and up the foothills to the east, this was an important commercial hub. On Father George's list of "must see attractions" was the bustling waterfront with its cafes, shops, and a clock made with plants and flowers that kept real time. There were multi-million-dollar yachts, car ferries, cruise ships, and freighters all going about their business. We found a table at an outdoor café facing the waterfront. The reader board in front advertised the "Best Moussaka in Greece." The dock provided a fascinating backdrop while we ate *moussaka* that did not disappoint. Over lunch, Father George looked over my papers.

Here I was with a Greek priest, on a Greek sidewalk, eating a Greek lunch, in the Greek city I was born. The scene was surreal. I didn't know what would happen next, but my instincts told me Father George was the right man to ask. Nervously I played with the olives in my salad, while I carefully watched his face for any reaction. After a few minutes, Father George looked up and commented, "This is interesting. It looks like you were born to a young woman out of wedlock and left at the Patras Orphanage when you were about ten days old. Your last name was Voukelatos. For an unmarried young woman, it would have been extremely tough to care for and support a baby, especially in those days."

"It is a sad story, but it explains how I ended up in the orphanage," I sighed.

Father continued, "I see the address of the orphanage on these papers. I wonder what happened to the place?"

"Thirty years is a long time; I'm sure it no longer exists. Nevertheless, I'd like to see where it stood," I replied.

"You're probably right. Maybe we could ask a resident if they remember where it was," Father concluded.

We were finishing our *moussaka* under the midday sun when an older man walked by our table. Father George greeted him and asked if he spoke English, which he did. Father asked if he remembered an orphanage on Sotiriadou Street. Pointing to his right, the man declared, "Yes, the orphanage is still there. Just drive to the top of the hill and follow the roundabout. It will be on your left; you can't miss it."

Had we heard the man correctly? Did he say the orphanage was still there after 30 years? In disbelief I shook my head, he couldn't possibly be thinking of the same place. Unprepared for his answer, he had piqued our curiosity enough that we wanted to see this place for ourselves. Unfortunately, our time was limited, so we agreed to wait until our next stop in Patras.

With time remaining, I fulfilled my dream of walking the streets of Patras. I strolled past coffee bars, browsed the shops, and bought a few souvenirs with "Patras" on them. I visited the pride of Patras, its flower clock, and yes, it accurately keeps the time. I walked towards the center of town to Plateia Giorgio, the largest square in the city. Home to the opera house and several marble fountains, it was a beautiful place to sit, and people watch. It didn't take me long to realize I was examining every face in hopes of finding someone who looked like me. It was silly, it was a long shot, but I couldn't help it. Soon I found myself taking in the sights as a daughter trying to see the city through her mother's eyes. *Had my mother ever sat and rested on this bench? Was this the grocery store where she shopped? What happened to her?*

Before I knew it, it was time to board the bus for the trip back to the I.V. When we were all on board Father George surprised everyone, especially me, when he announced our bus would be making a brief detour. He told the group I had lived in a Patras orphanage 30 years ago, and we were going to check if the address on my adoption papers and the orphanage were the same. Andonis, our driver, was in on the plan. No one minded the short delay; in fact, everyone was excited and wished me luck.

Deftly, Andonis maneuvered the large bus up the steep, narrow, street that ran through the center of town. He followed the roundabout onto Sotiriadou Street and stopped in front of a three-story building that filled the entire block. Most of the cream-colored paint had worn away, revealing gray cement walls. Two ornate wrought iron doors created the entrance, which led to a small courtyard. Behind the right door stood a giant baby carriage with spoked wheels and a yellow hood. The iron had been designed to leave an opening large enough to pass a baby through. To the right of the doors on the outside wall was a door-bell. *Had young mothers placed their babies in the carriage, rung the bell and slipped away? Was this where I was left?*

As Father George and I stepped off the bus, I was moving in slow motion. Had he just hijacked an entire bus full of people on my behalf? We passed through the iron gates and entered the courtyard where a garden of yellow flowers surrounded terra cotta statues of the Virgin Mary and four small children. Andonis, who left his bus and took charge of the situation, quickly found a caretaker who told us the director, Mr. Alivizatos, was on vacation for a week.

The caretaker confirmed this was the same address listed on my papers but surprised us when he said this was not the same building where I had lived. The first orphanage, built in the late 1800s, had served the city for almost 100 years. In the late 1960s, it was razed, and a new orphanage opened in 1972. Hearing the squeals and laughter of children at play above us, I inquired about the noise. The man explained the new building served two purposes. It was still a home for orphaned babies, but it also served as a kindergarten school during the day.

He permitted us to walk around, so we headed to the second floor where we found several classrooms and the playground. The rooms looked like those in a typical school, with desks, chairs, books, and chalkboards. The play area was covered with gravel and sand but had a swing set and monkey bars. Down the hall past the classrooms, we found a room with eight cribs, each holding a baby. These were the orphans. When I asked about the small number, he said there were a few older children, but they lived in foster homes. The orphanage was paying for their care. The babies looked well cared for, but I wondered how often they were held and comforted. Looking at the tiny bundles swaddled in blankets filled me with great sadness. Long ago, I was one of these babies. I felt a profound connection to them, and for a moment, it took all my self-control not to grab one of those sweet bundles and make a break for the door. Like Ellen, I knew I could give a baby a loving home. Better judgment prevailed but turning my back on those cribs took every bit of emotional resolve I possessed. There would be no Refugee Relief Act to facilitate an adoption for them. Their fate rested in the hands of their fellow Greeks.

On our way out, I saw a picture of the Gerber baby on a wall. It stopped me dead in my tracks. *My Susie doll was in the Patras orphanage?! I wondered if that picture had hung inside the original building. If so, had I seen it as a child? When I received the same doll in San Diego, had it triggered a memory and comforted me?* I didn't have any answers, but I took that picture as another sign I had made this trip at the right time. There was something important happening here I needed to record, so I started a daily journal. Thanking the caretaker, we made plans to return when the director was back from vacation.

Back on the bus, Father George announced, "This is the place. Maria lived here." Loud cheering and clapping erupted from my fellow travelers. Overwhelmed, I found my seat, rested my forehead on the seatback in front of me, and tried to wrap my head around the enormity of our discovery.

THE BOOK OF REVELATIONS

PREFERRING TO BE ALONE WITH MY THOUGHTS, I DIDN'T talk much on the drive back to I.V. Everything had happened so fast I could barely make sense of it all. It was remarkable, yet sad Patras still had an orphanage after 30 years. Learning I had not lived in the building I saw today was a big revelation and piqued my interest in the original structure. Even more important to me was whether the records from the 1950s had survived the move to the new place. I didn't hold out much hope, but I looked forward to my next meeting with Mr. Alivizatos. I would get my chance sooner than later as Patras was north of the Ionian Village. We would pass through it several times on our way to and from our various destinations.

We spent two days back at the I.V. before we hit the road again. With Andonis at the wheel, we drove from one end of Greece to another. We crossed over rugged mountains on winding roads, traversed fertile plains, and hugged a crooked coastline of endless beaches. We visited all the well-known ancient sites like Olympia, Sparta, and Delphi, and a few lesser-known ones like Kalavryta, Methoni, and Lamia. Our trip took us to the northern city of Thessaloniki to visit the Alexander the Great exhibit before it left on a U.S. tour. While strolling on the waterfront, our group ran into Father Paul, a classmate of Father George's from Boston's Holy Cross School of Theology. Father Paul was completing his graduate degree at the local university and didn't know Father George was even in Greece. While the others toured the waterfront, Father George introduced me to Father Paul and told him about my connection to the Patras Orphanage. He added I would be returning to Patras after my time at the Ionian Village. Father Paul, who was spending July in Patras with his wife's family, gave me his telephone number and said to call when I was back in town. I didn't know it then, but I had just made another life-changing connection.

With Father George and Father Tom as our guides, we experienced Greece in a way few people do. Their knowledge of the Greek people, Greek language and culture, as well as of the country itself, made it possible to experience the *real* Greece. In the picturesque *choria* (villages) Greece came alive for us with ancient customs, exceptional food and warm hospitality. We danced the *tsamikos*, tried singing along with a few traditional songs, and sampled *tsipouro*, a bold drink first made by monks in the 14th century. I thoroughly enjoyed those evenings in the villages, but I always felt a little uneasy. Lingering in the back of my mind was the image of another *real* Greece: The poor, shattered Greece where desperate mothers with few resources gave up their children to be sent out of the country and raised by strangers.

My next visit to Patras came on the return trip from the World War II memorial at Kalavryta. The group had stopped in downtown Patras for a couple of hours to buy snacks and stretch our legs. Father George and I had other plans. We took a cab to the orphanage with the hope of finding the director back from his vacation. We entered the courtyard and were greeted by a young man with a friendly smile who spoke decent English. He introduced himself as Mr. Alivizatos and ushered us into his office. He had heard about our earlier visit and was eager to help.

His office was a sparsely furnished room with an old wooden desk, square table, two rickety chairs, and a small closet. As I took in the stark surroundings, my eyes came to rest on a beautiful old icon depicting a saint sitting among several small children. "Saint Nicholas is the patron saint of children," explained Mr. Alivizatos. I thought it was beautiful and it comforted me to see it in this place.

I got to the point and told Mr. Alivizatos I was left in the "Baby Receiver" at this address. I showed him my paperwork, which proved this was the right place. Mr. Alivizatos reminded us the current building had replaced the first orphanage, but everything had been saved and moved into the new one. It was a long shot, but I also asked him if he knew Mr. Londos, the director who might have met my birth mother in 1953. He said he regretted never meeting Mr. Londos personally, but knew of his excellent reputation. He had been the director during WWII and through the Civil War. Those were dark days for Greece, but from what he'd seen, Mr. Londos kept excellent records. Every abandoned baby was registered in a ledger the day it arrived, and any personal items left by the mothers were saved. When the overseas adoptions started, Mr. Londos played a pivotal role in selecting which children went to America. A decent man and competent director, it must have been a demanding, heart-wrenching, responsibility for him.

Until now, I thought I had seen everything related to my adoption, so I asked him, "Do I have a ledger entry? My papers say my name was Voukelatos, and I was left here on May 13th, 1953." I watched as Mr. Alivizatos walked over to the small closet and returned with an over-sized book.

"We'll know soon enough," he stated.

At first glance, the book with 1953 on the cover, looked like an old accounting ledger with worn leather corners and spine. The cover boards were sheathed in a dull-gray fabric and stitched together with bindery cord. Mr. Alivizatos explained the nurse who retrieved the baby was responsible for recording any information about the child left that day. He leafed through the book until he came to the page for May 13th. Smiling, he said, "Here is your name, Maria Voukelatos. The first column was filled in by the nurse who found you." Turning the book toward me so I could see the entry for myself, he translated from the Greek:

Maria was left in the baby receiver at 10:30 p.m. on 13 May 1953 when approximately ten days old. She was wearing a white hat and jumper with a note pinned to her clothes. Another paper from the City Hall was found tucked into her blanket.

Here, at last, was a fragile connection to my birth mother. Gently, I moved my fingers over the faded blue ink as if doing so might somehow transport me back to that day in the spring of 1953. Father George and I were caught up in the moment and not prepared for the director's next question, "Would you like to see the note?"

Like the week before, I found myself questioning my hearing. "A note from whom?" I asked.

"From your mother! She left it with you in the baby receiver," Mr. Alivizatos replied.

"Yes, Yes, I would!" I replied.

There, written in pencil on thin, faded paper was a tangible bond to my mother. The writing was sizeable, almost childlike, and the paper had been placed on a rough surface when written. I couldn't read Greek, but I noticed the note was signed. When I asked about the signature, Mr. Alivizatos answered, "That is your mother's name, Hariklea Voukelatos." I couldn't believe what I was seeing. After all these years, my birth mother's handwriting was right there in front of me. My head was spinning as I looked for a place to sit. Thankfully Father George helped me to a chair, took the note, and waited. When I was ready, he translated for me:

I have the honor to ask you to take my little girl, and maybe God will make me worthy to take her back later because right now I am merely worthy of pity and am very unfortunate. I have baptized her with the name Maria.

Hariklea Voukelatos
Patras, 13 May 1953

In a split second, that note changed everything. Learning my birth mother's name made her a real person. Mr. Alivizatos told me Hariklea's name translated to Harriet in English. I liked Harriet. It was a robust, sturdy name – one you could count on. Growing up, I'd never thought of myself as being "born" only "adopted." That was no longer true; I was "born" to Hariklea Voukelatos. She named me, baptized me, and left me in a safe place. She had cared about me.

Returning to the ledger, Mr. Alivizatos handed me another piece of paper left in the receiver. "Your mother, Hariklea, was an extraordinary woman. She went to great lengths to take additional precautions I've never seen done before. She filed a declaration, an oral statement in her case, with the mayor's office in the City Hall of Patras. There she explained her desperate situation in detail and requested the orphanage take over your care."

Looking at the official document, the first thing I noticed were the stamps along the top. Mr. Alivizatos explained the paper had cost

Hariklea three drachmas to file, a low-wage workers' pay for three hours of work back then. My next question concerned an unfamiliar name, Efstathios. "Is that my grandfather's name?" I asked.

"Yes, it is. It's a name you probably wouldn't have learned if Hariklea had not filed this paper. Proper Greek documents required the petitioner to state his or her father's name as well." As I looked on, Mr. Alivizatos translated:

Declaration to the City Hall
Petition of Hariklea Voukelatos
Daughter of Efstathios
A resident of Patras 13 May 1953
To Mr. Mayor of Patras:

I have the honor to tell you I have acquired a 10-day-old female child out of wedlock. Because I happened to be without protection and paralyzed in my right leg, poor, without any means, and ill, I cannot protect the child. Therefore, I request you to act as you see fit, and I enter this child into the Patras Orphanage for its protection; otherwise, the newborn child will die. With all respect, the person filing this request is illiterate. Hariklea Voukelatos

Here was more proof Hariklea's decision to give me up had not been easy or made in haste. Her heart must have been breaking as she sat in the City Hall and arranged to give up her child. Leaving me at the orphanage had been her solution of last resort. Finding the orphanage was big; finding the note was huge. But finding the declaration was monumental because it provided me with insight into Hariklea's state of mind. She was brave, determined, and despite her ordeal, had taken precautions to ensure I would survive. She had loved me, and I could not love her back.

With this new information came more questions. *What was wrong with Hariklea's right foot? What did "without protection" mean? After all the expense and trouble, why hadn't she come back for me?* Only something catastrophic would have prevented her from retrieving me. So, I embraced the only conclusion that made sense: Hariklea must have been killed in an accident or died from an illness. I was heartsick, I would never get to meet her, but knowing she had loved me was a priceless gift.

When I asked Mr. Alivizatos if I could have the two documents, he gently refused, stating they were the property of the Greek State. Instead, he offered to make copies I could pick up after the I.V. trip was over, and I returned with Father Paul. I thanked Mr. Alivizatos for his openness, time, and the priceless paperwork he found. That meeting changed my life forever.

Father George and I caught a cab back to the waterfront. With time to spare before we were due back on the bus, I found a bench and reflected on the informative visit! I had no idea the orphanage kept such excellent records. One hour ago, the only thing I knew was my Greek name. Now I knew my exact birthdate, my birth mother's name and circumstances, and my grandfather's name. But without a doubt, the most important gift I received today was learning about Hariklea and her love for me.

Back on the bus, Father George shared the highlights of our visit. Again, his news was met with enthusiastic cheers. "You folks are certainly getting more than your money's worth on this tour," Father George joked. Everyone was surprised at the orphanage's meticulous record-keeping and the care its staff had given to the artifacts left with the babies. My friends wanted to know what I was going to do next, but I didn't have much of an answer for them. The only thing I knew for sure; I was returning to Patras after I.V. to pick up the copies Mr. Alivizatos made for me.

In the 1980s, adoption information was easy to get. The baby ledgers rested on a table in the director's office for easy viewing. Staff members enjoyed helping adult adoptees find their entries and items left with them. Years later, one of the rooms was transformed into a museum/memorial. Tall wooden cases displayed children's clothes and toys. A doctor's medical bag sat on a shelf near the copper baptismal basin. A long, glass-covered table protected copies of notes left by bereft mothers long ago. Mounted on the wall was a large, decorative, hook that held charms and icons left with the babies. The room was a powerful reminder of Greece's troubled past and the children affected by those hard times.

Sadly, laws and local practices changed in the late 1990s, and it became hard for adoptees to access their information. The ledgers were secreted away in lawyer's offices, and all artifacts in the memorial room were removed. There are a few pieces of furniture, a typewriter, and a baptismal font crammed together at the end of a dark hallway, but no evidence the building on Sotiriadou street housed orphaned children. Today the building serves one purpose, a school. In my case, the timing was everything.

ON MY OWN

THE DAYS FLEW BY, AND BEFORE WE KNEW IT, OUR IONIAN Village trip had come to an end. In the month we spent together we learned about orthodoxy, Greece, and each other. We had started this trip as strangers from all over North America and become friends. Life-long friendships were made that summer as we traveled from one end of the country to the other. There were museums, churches, beaches, and tavernas. Some of our group became good Greek dancers by the end of our stay.

Andonis drove us back to Athens for our final night together. Tomorrow we would visit the Parthenon and go our separate ways, each acutely aware we had shared a real highlight of our lives. Those who were leaving Greece talked of the future: back to work for some, another month of summer vacation for others. Those who were staying made plans to visit relatives or more ancient sites. Father George and Father Tom were heading back to I.V. for the next camp session: high school kids. God bless them! I was going to visit a couple of islands with some I.V. friends and then return to Patras alone.

We checked into our last hotel that afternoon and ate a light supper together. The roof of the Hotel Balasca was the site of our 1984 Adult Session Farewell Party. With the Acropolis as a backdrop, we reminisced and shared stories about the days and weeks we had spent together. We posed for a group photo and listened to some parting words from Father George and Father Tom. I was surprised when Father George shared my story had added an unexpected dynamic to the group spirit. All my I.V. friends knew about the AHEPA, but none had heard of the 1950s adoption program or its Refugee Relief Committee. Finding the orphanage after 30 years was remarkable, but the real story was how I came to live in America and how my adoption shed light on an episode of Greek history. Born in a postwar Greece rife with poverty and despair, I was saved by a Greece that mercifully gave up its precious children rather than let them die. Father George was pleased I had illuminated a dark period in Greek history and embodied its positive outcome.

The following morning would bring organized chaos as everyone checked out of their rooms, so most of us said our goodbyes at the party. There were hugs, kisses, and tears as we promised to keep in touch. Friends expressed their delight over learning more Greek history and wished me luck on my return to Patras. I saved my last goodbye for Father George, but the words caught in my throat. I hugged him and managed a raspy, "thank you for everything." He wished me luck when I returned to Patras.

We rose early and arrived at the foot of the Acropolis just as it opened. It took more physical effort than I expected to reach the top of this massive hill of rock. My short legs complained as I climbed the steep steps. My lungs protested too. As I struggled to catch my breath, I rested and took in the panoramic view of Athens, a city of four million people spreading out from the Acropolis for as far as I could see.

Approaching the Parthenon, I saw scaffolding on two sides and a tower crane in the center. The Greeks were trying to reverse the extensive damage done to the marble by decades of air pollution. Even with the visual distractions, the Parthenon was a colossal marble structure. The columns alone were massive creations, each one was six feet in diameter, and there were 48 of them. The temple no longer had a roof, only intricately carved gables at each end. I was sure I asked the same question every visitor did, how had the ancient Greeks built this?

The guards providing security on top of the Acropolis were not what I expected either. Tourists taking marble rocks as souvenirs was a real problem. The guards carried guns, but their real weapons were whistles, which they blew if anyone was seen picking up a rock or even bending over too far. A whistle blast was followed by guards running, a demand to explain yourself, and glares from the other tourists. It didn't take long to figure out what to do and what not to do. I made sure all my possessions were buttoned up and secured because heaven help me if I dropped anything. I was not going to be one of *those* tourists. In this case, humiliation was an effective deterrent.

At that moment, it struck me I was walking in the footsteps of ancient Athenians who had lived thousands of years ago. Had an ancient ancestor of mine stood here? It was heady stuff. Until I came to Greece, my only experience with antiquities had been in museums. Walking around a structure this old was difficult for me to comprehend, so I found a bench and basked in the history.

Sitting there, I let my memories float like the wispy cirrus clouds overhead. I loved that Greece's most famous symbol was built to honor a woman, the goddess Athena. I thought about my two earlier attempts to visit Greece and was glad they had not worked out. On both attempts, friends had canceled due to work conflicts. This was a better trip! I thought about Mom back home in America, and how thrilled she was for me. Last, but not least, I thought about my third-grade report on Greece and smiled. My childhood dream had come true.

Still on cloud nine after my visit to the Parthenon, I headed to the port with Stacy and Georgia to catch a ferry to Mykonos and Santorini. Both were two of Greece's best-known islands. Popular Mykonos, known for its white-washed houses and quaint windmills, was our first stop. Pulling up to the dock, I was surprised to see a group of men and women holding up photographs of various sizes. We disembarked and were immediately surrounded by boisterous owners hawking their hotels like fishmongers. "Come, come, stay here, let me show you, I have the best rooms," they shouted. It took us a minute to find our bearings and figure out we were supposed to look at the photos and make a lodging selection. We chose a hotel on a beach from a gorgeous specimen named Stefanos. We chose *him* as much as we chose his hotel. Well, scenery is scenery. We followed Stefanos to his small truck where he stowed our luggage, along with us, and off we went.

As we drove, I was surprised at how stark the Aegean island landscape looked compared to the lush green of the Ionian Islands to the west. This barren place resembled the surface of the moon, save for the adorable windmills that looked like they had been placed there by some Hollywood set designer. Stefanos' photos did not disappoint. His hotel was charming, and we spent a quiet week right on the beach. After days of keeping a busy daily schedule, it was nice to relax with nowhere to go. We didn't rent a car or scooters, so our sightseeing excursions were limited. When we needed to go into town, we hitchhiked on the backs of motorcycles. It was 1984, and we didn't think twice about it.

For almost a week, our only decisions were towel placement for maximum sun exposure and what to eat. I loved trying the various dishes served in the beach tavernas. We always ordered a Greek salad along with the main dish. *Pastitsio*, a staple of Greek cuisine, became a fast favorite of mine. It resembles lasagna and can be made in many ways. I ordered mine with meat. As I ate, I wondered if Hariklea made her *pastitsio* the same way. Did she use a secret recipe or spice handed down from *her* mother? Greek salads were another matter entirely. As I mined my salad for the cucumbers, I wondered what Hariklea would think of a daughter who disliked tomatoes, olives, and feta!

Rested and energized, we headed south for a week on Santorini. As our ferry approached the dock, my immediate impression was this island was unlike any other. Santorini was as dramatic as Mykonos was quaint. More than three millennia ago, the island was the round mountain top of an active volcano. A massive eruption hurled the top of the volcano into the air and carved out a caldera rimmed by massive cliffs. White-washed houses sat on the edge and spilled down as if covering them in snow.

On the dock, we were again mobbed by hotel owners holding up pictures, but by now we knew the drill. We selected an affordable hotel from another handsome Greek named Mitsos. There seemed to be a pattern developing in our hotel selections. We piled into his car and zigzagged up the steep face of the cliff. Our lives passed before us more than once as we made one sharp hairpin turn after another on the narrow road with oncoming traffic. When we reached the top of the cliff, we finally dared to open our eyes and admire the landscape again. We drove about a mile inland and arrived at the Spartan Hotel. The rooms were airy and decorated in "tourist Greek" with hand-made furniture. Mopeds were available to rent, so we were in business.

We began our first day at the famous black sand beach, but it was empty: too hot to lay on and too hot to walk on. Picturesque churches with white crosses and blue domes dominated every town and village. The shops were divine, but pricey even back in 1984. One day we were headed to the southern tip of the island to visit a large archeological site when we spied an amusing sign: "Real Virgin Wine Not Sold Before Its Time." We stopped and were greeted by Manolos, the jolly winemaker who insisted we sample his latest batch of red wine. His wife, Maria, brought out a plate of local fare and before long we were eating, drinking and laughing like family. We never did learn what made wine "virgin," but the afternoon provided a beautiful peek at family life on Santorini.

Of course, the highlight of any trip to Santorini is watching the sunset from a terrace cafe in the village of Oia, overlooking the Aegean. Enjoying a glass or two of local wine, we reminisced about our time on Greece's most beautiful islands. Eventually, the discussion turned to the subject of our next destinations. My I.V. friends were headed to the island of Rhodes for more fun in the sun, and I was returning to the mainland, where I had some unfinished business.

THE THIRD DOOR

BEFORE I LEFT SANTORINI, I CALLED FATHER PAUL AND told him I would be in Patras in a couple of days. I shared with him the highlights of my visit with Mr. Alivizatos and the treasures we found in the ledger. He was shocked to learn such papers even existed and pleased Mr. Alivizatos had offered to make copies for me.

The ferry ride was uneventful and on time. I arrived in Athens and headed to the train station for the three-hour trip to Patras. It was a busy time, and the train was packed, so I stood up the entire time. With time to think, I wondered what awaited me in Patras. I was excited to see the copies Mr. Alivizatos made for me, and spend time with people who knew the city well.

My aching feet and I checked into the Acropolis Hotel where I phoned Father Paul and was happy to learn he had stopped by the orphanage and picked up copies of Hariklea's note and the City Hall declaration. I thanked him and mentioned if possible, I would like to get a copy of my baptismal record while I was in Greece. If I wanted to get married in the Greek Orthodox Church, I would need it. Father Paul agreed and said our first stop would be the City Hall.

Father Paul and his wife, Evi, collected me the next morning, and we headed downtown. Evi and I waited outside while Father Paul went into the records office at the City Hall. The place was bustling with people as they conducted their business with the city. Watching the never-ending stream of people, I wondered if this was the same place Hariklea had come 30 years earlier to file her declaration before she left me at the orphanage. Father Paul returned empty-handed. My baptismal record was not there, and the clerk had no idea where it might be. For now, it looked like I had reached a dead end.

Disappointed but not disheartened, we stopped for coffee and studied the copies from the orphanage. We had three names: my grandfather Efstathios, my birth mother Hariklea, and Voukelatos, my surname. Evi, a native of Patras, explained sometimes it was possible to tell what part of Greece a person was from by their family name. Greeks didn't move often, and those who did leave their small villages for the city tried to relocate near people who came from the same area. There was a neighborhood called Synora where people with surnames like Voukelatos lived. Many of the people who lived there were from the islands off Greece's western coast.

I asked, "Since my mother is not alive, maybe we could find someone who knew my grandfather. Finding information about a blood relative would mean a lot to me. Would you mind giving it a try?"

They agreed, so we finished our coffees and headed for Synora to see if we could find anyone who knew Efstathios Voukelatos. We drove a good 15 minutes and then turned down an empty street. We could have been anywhere in Patras for all I knew. We parked in the middle of the block and walked to the corner house. Typical of homes in the area, it was white with a matching door and shutters. Father Paul knocked on the door while Evi and I stood behind him. I hoped his clerical collar would make people less suspicious and more willing to talk. A youngish woman answered the door, but the conversation was brief. She said she didn't know anyone named Voukelatos. The same happened with the middle-aged man next door. At the third door, a middle-aged woman answered. As we waited, Evi and I were expecting the same response. Instead, the conversation sped up and continued, on and on. Confused, I looked from Father Paul to Evi and saw tears flowing down her cheeks.

"What's going on?" I pleaded.

Evi whispered, "This woman doesn't know your grandfather, but she knows your mother, Hariklea. She said she is alive and working nearby today. She works for the city cleaning the public restrooms. It's a good job and comes with a pension. This woman says you can go there and see her now."

My mother was alive and living in Patras?! My head was spinning; there must be some mistake. The woman from the neighborhood must be thinking of a different Hariklea Voukelatos. You don't find your birth mother after 30 years by knocking on a few doors. As I tried to make sense of this new information, my mind raced for a way to confirm this was the right Hariklea. Suddenly I remembered the paper Hariklea had filed at the City Hall mentioned she was crippled. I suggested Father Paul ask the woman if *her* Hariklea was disabled in any way. "Yes," she replied, "she wears a special shoe on her right foot." I was surprised, but not convinced. Everything I had seen proved the woman we sought would have returned for her child. Still, I could not ignore the similarities between the two women. We needed to find this Hariklea and learn her story. The result might change two people's lives forever.

Over lunch, we discussed the possible scenarios. If this woman was my birth mother, would she want her past revived? Maybe I was the result of a mistake she had made when she was a young woman. Having that "mistake" show up 30 years later might be a horrible intrusion into her life, and I was uncomfortable asking a stranger if she had given up a baby. If she had kept my birth a secret all this time, the consequences of my return could be devastating. On the other hand, what if Hariklea had been looking for her daughter all these years? Finding her child would be the answer to her prayers.

Over a quick lunch, my friends and I prayed for wisdom and guidance on how to handle this delicate situation. We decided Father Paul and Evi would approach the woman without me while I watched from nearby. We wanted to meet her before she left for the day and the afternoon siesta began, so we started walking. With the July heat above the century mark, no one was outside except a few patrons dining in the nearby restaurants. We found the bathrooms halfway down a steep, narrow, street filled with eateries and almost obscured by a massive oak tree. I saw a figure moving about inside, but the intricate shadows made it difficult to see much. I spied a restaurant balcony across the street where I could watch the scene unfold, so I made my way upstairs. From that distance, I couldn't see or hear anything until the three of them walked outside. As I stared at Hariklea, it was apparent something was wrong with her right foot, which caused a distinct limp. What was not obvious was any physical similarity to me. I watched as Father Paul quietly continued to question her.

Unexpectedly, like a flip had switched, her demeanor changed, and she became agitated and upset. Her loud, angry, voice caught the attention of nearby diners who wandered outside to see what all the fuss was about. I didn't need to understand Greek to realize she had denied having a baby and was furious anyone, especially strangers, would ask such a question. I was unnerved and felt terrible about the scene I was witnessing. Had we made the right decision in coming here? Father Paul and Evi, unprepared for such a violent outburst began retreating when Hariklea demanded, "Where is this woman you say is my daughter? I want to meet her. Bring her here this minute!"

By now, a substantial crowd had gathered, and I was startled when Father Paul motioned for me to come down. As I approached the group, all eyes were on Hariklea and me. My heart was pounding as the strangers encircled us and closed in, studying our faces from just inches away. Some pointed and nodded, others pointed and shook their heads. All experts in facial recognition and hereditary features, everyone had an opinion on whether Hariklea was my mother. I looked directly at her, but she showed no sign of recognition. Father Paul gently handed her the copy of the note left with me at the orphanage and asked if she recognized it. Her face was completely blank and showed no emotion. Not one vein bulged, not one muscle twitched. We had approached the wrong woman, or she was the best actress I had ever seen.

I was sure we'd made a terrible mistake and approached the wrong woman. In Greek, I apologized for the intrusion and thanked her as best I could. While I spoke, I tried to memorize every inch of her face from her curly white hair, dark eyes, and skin, to her button nose. If this Hariklea was my mother, she had chosen and deserved her privacy. Disappointed, we apologized once more and started back up the hill. We had taken a few steps when Hariklea asked Father Paul for his telephone number. She said she knew a woman who might be able to help us with our search for the right Hariklea and would call later with more information.

Back at Father Paul and Evi's house, we discussed what had happened. None of us believed we had found the right Hariklea. Her lack of emotion when shown the note convinced us we met the wrong woman. Siesta time came and went, but I did not rest. I held out hope Hariklea would call with important news. At 5:00 p.m. she called and asked to meet us in two hours at a specific table in Plateia Psilalonia, a public square. She said she had information that might help us find *my* Hariklea. At 6:45 p.m., Father Paul, Evi, and I were waiting. From the dense foliage surrounding us, we understood she wanted her privacy, but her need for secrecy worried me, and I began to sweat. At 7:00 p.m., sharp Hariklea appeared through the bushes and sat down. Without any introduction, she looked directly into my eyes and stated, "Είμαι η μητέρα σου και αυτό είναι ακριβώς σαν τις ταινίες."

I looked to Father Paul and Evi for a translation but saw expressions that could only be described as astonished. Father Paul's jaw hung open, and Evi was crying. I looked from one to the other and then back again. The silence was deafening. At last, Father Paul turned and told me Hariklea had said: "I am your mother, and this is just like the movies." It took more than a moment for her comment to register with me. The woman we met earlier was my birth mother, and she had been in Patras all this time?! When I could finally speak, I took a couple of deep breaths and whispered the words I had waited a lifetime to say: "You never came back for me. Please help me understand what happened to you."

Daubing the sweat from her brow and drinking her entire bottle of water, she took her time composing herself. When she was ready, Hariklea briefly described what happened to her 30 years ago.

THE DAUGHTER OF EFSTATHIOS

HARIKLEA VOUKELATOS WAS FROM A SMALL VILLAGE ON a small Ionian island off the western coast of Greece. When she was six-years-old, her mother, Zoe, died. At seven she contracted polio that paralyzed her right foot. Unmarried and pregnant at 16, she was forced to leave her village for Patras. She gave birth to me on May 3rd, 1953, but it wasn't long before she realized she could not care for me. With no job or family support, she had no option but to place me in the local orphanage until her situation improved. Three years later, her circumstances were no better, and she lost me through adoption to an American couple.

Through tears of regret, Hariklea finished. "It broke my heart, but I agreed to let you go so you could have a better life. All these years, I knew I had a daughter in America, and I have never forgotten about you. After you left, I took a job in a furniture factory where I met a good man and had another daughter, Katina. My husband died when she was just ten. I have been working for the city of Patras and raising my daughter since then."

Father Paul asked her why she had denied knowing me earlier that day, especially when he had given her the note to read. Her reasons came as a surprise. Hariklea was illiterate. She could barely write her name and could not read at all. The paper was just a series of marks on a page. Also, Hariklea had seen a man from her island, Lefkada, standing in the crowd, and she was frightened he would learn about me.

Her next comment gave me goosebumps. Hariklea told me while inside the restroom, she had heard a noise, looked up, and there I was at the top of the hill after almost 30 years! I asked her how she knew it was me. She did not offer any specific reason but replied, "You are my child, and a mother always knows her child."

A silence fell over the table as we reflected on Hariklea's story. It must have taken superhuman strength to control herself when she saw me. How tragic social control, after all those years, still conditioned her behavior to the degree she had renounced her child rather than be exposed. If she had not responded with the anger of fear and panic, perhaps Hariklea's initial response would have been more in line with my expectations about a reunion with my birth mother. But Hariklea was her own person, and I was fast getting to know just how strong-willed she was.

When Hariklea invited me to spend a few days with her and Katina, I quickly agreed. I didn't care if I spoke enough Greek. *My* Hariklea had invited me to stay in her home. She asked I arrive at 6:00 the next evening so she could prepare Katina. She didn't want her 18-year-old daughter to know what had happened to her when she was 15, so she asked I tell everyone I was a cousin from America on her father's side. Her joy, tempered with concern for her daughter's feelings, gave me another glimpse of Hariklea's decent character.

With our plans finalized, we parted ways in the park, and Father Paul and Evi took me to my hotel for the night. We were going to spend tomorrow together and head to Hariklea's house in the evening. Lying on the bed, I recounted the day's events. I had to admit I had a few questions after our first meeting. Hariklea had not mentioned the man who got her pregnant, my birth father. *What happened between those two? What was his name, and where was he?* I didn't want to be intrusive, so I let it go. There would be time for the tough questions later.

I could have done with less drama, but we had found the right Hariklea after all. Learning she had never stopped thinking of me touched me deeply but left me troubled. Knowing her child was far away and being raised by strangers must have been 30 years of hell. God only knows how Hariklea survived a loss like that, but he had shown his hand, and tomorrow night, I would be sleeping in her home. As I drifted off to sleep, I'm sure there was a smile on my face.

The following morning, Father Paul and Evi picked me up, and the three of us headed downtown to run a few errands. As we shopped for fresh bread and veggies, I felt lighter and more carefree. For the first time, I could soak up the vitality of Patras life without staring at every face, looking for someone who resembled me. By the time we finished, it was mid-day, so we headed back to Father Paul and Evi's house for lunch and rest. Unable to relax, my mind raced with questions and anticipation. *Had Hariklea's talk with Katina gone well? Would Katina believe I was a cousin from America? If not Hariklea, then who had written the note placed with me in the baby receiver?*

Anxious and giddy, I climbed into the back seat of Father Paul and Evi's car at 5:30 p.m. With Father Paul at the wheel and Evi riding shotgun, we returned to Synora where we had found Hariklea. Not far from those public restrooms, Father Paul pulled up in front of a small, one-story cinder-block home. Hariklea came out to greet us, followed by a pretty, petite, girl with black hair hanging down to her waist.

Wearing turquoise shorts with a black tank top, she looked confused as she stared at the strange visitors. She must be my half-sister, Katina. Father Paul introduced me as an American cousin from Hariklea's father's side of the family. Katina didn't react but greeted me warmly in English. I breathed a sigh of relief as she grabbed my suitcase and went inside. I bid farewell to Father Paul and Evi with the promise of saying goodbye before I returned to the States. They had taken on my search in Patras and made it successful. I could never thank them enough for the gift they gave me. I took comfort in knowing we shared a connection that would last a lifetime.

Inside Hariklea's house, the first thing I noticed was how sparsely the home was furnished. Cleaning restrooms for the city might be a good job, but she was still poor. There was a sitting room, a tiny kitchen, and a bathroom. The floors were cold cement, and the walls were bare except for the Orthodox shrine holding a candle and religious icons. The house was so small one of the beds was stuffed into the kitchen, wedged in between the refrigerator and the counter. Katina informed me I was sleeping in the kitchen while they shared the fold-out couch in the sitting room. I stowed my suitcase under the bed, put on my PJs, and slid between the crisp sheets.

Lying there, listening to the steady hum of the refrigerator, I reflected on the enormity of the past two days. Finding my birth mother on my second day in Patras was so implausible, I still had trouble believing it. Lying no more than 15 feet away in the next room, I wondered what Hariklea was thinking as her head hit the pillow? Her prayers had been answered when the child she lost returned to Greece and found her. I had no doubt, being blessed with a second chance to know each other put a smile on both our sleepy faces.

Many adoptees who search for a parent spend thousands of dollars and many years in their quest. Some have success and reunite with family. Others locate a parent only to discover he or she has died, and many find nothing at all, not even simple information like a firm date of birth. Finally, there are those who find a parent only to endure soul-crushing rejection. Surely God's hand was evident in *my* discovery.

AGAIN, I AM MARIA VOUKELATOS

I WAS AWAKENED EARLY BY THE SOUND OF FEET SHUF-
fling unevenly across the kitchen floor. Disoriented at first, it took
me a moment to remember I was in Hariklea's home. My kitchen bed
was more comfortable than I expected, just the right size for my 5'2"
frame. Feeling rested, I sat up and watched Hariklea unwrap pieces of
spanakopita (spinach pie), arrange them on a plate, and set the table for
breakfast. Rich smelling coffee was already percolating on the countertop propane burner.

Waking up in my birth mother's home, I was excited to see what
the day would bring. While Katina slept, Hariklea and I enjoyed our
first breakfast together as mother and daughter. The conversation
was limited to small talk, nods, and headshakes, but we didn't mind.
Reunited after so many years, I am sure neither of us ever imagined
such a day. A week ago, I hadn't known Hariklea was alive. Separated by
thousands of miles for decades, I could scarcely believe I was sitting in
her home! If anyone had suggested such a thing, I would have laughed

in their face. Thrust into a surreal situation, I had to pinch myself to make sure this was not a dream. Hariklea was right; this was just like the movies.

Over breakfast, I studied Hariklea's face. We shared identical hairlines, but that was all. Her upturned nose, small eyes, and mouth did not resemble mine as I recalled the opinionated crowd that encircled us two days ago. Even they could not agree on any physical resemblances between us. None of that mattered now. Hariklea had admitted the truth to me, and we had the rest of our lives to discover each other.

Katina awoke and entered the kitchen, rubbing the sleep from her eyes. Her thick long hair was wildly messy and gave her an exotic look. She gave me a quizzical glance as if she had forgotten they had a house guest and joined us at the table. There was light conversation while Katina ate the last of the *spanakopita* and we sipped another cup of coffee.

When Katina finished, we cleaned up the kitchen, made the beds, and showered. After the chores, Hariklea announced we were all taking a taxi downtown to go shopping. Polio made walking difficult and driving impossible for Hariklea, so she used taxis to get around. As we strolled past the busy shops, I watched her navigate the uneven curbs and sidewalks. The black leather boot with its three-inch rubber sole was scuffed and worn with age. There were no expensive braces on the sides to support her paralyzed ankle, so her foot flopped to one side when she walked. Hariklea's limp was severe, but she managed the uneven surfaces of the city streets with skill. Wanting to protect her, I stayed close just in case.

Up ahead was a market where we could shop for extra groceries, so I was taken aback when Hariklea entered a jewelry store. Katina and I watched as she examined the fancy baubles under the glass counter and selected a gold necklace with a small pendant. The size of a dime, it was edged with the classical Greek key design with a small diamond in the center. What was Hariklea doing? I looked to Katina for an answer, but she looked confused as well. Before she took out her wallet, Hariklea turned and handed me the necklace. I gently pushed it away. I could not accept such an expensive gift, but no amount of pleading would change her mind. The jeweler spoke English, so I asked him to explain I could not accept something so extravagant. He pulled me aside and whispered she felt incredibly guilty about *something*, and it was best if I took the necklace. I knew better than to argue any longer, so I put it on and thanked her for the special gift.

We left the jewelry shop and found our way to a large department store where Hariklea bought me a pink nightgown. I had pajamas with me, but I guess she felt I needed some from Patras. I was quickly learning Hariklea did not take "no" for an answer, so I accepted the nightgown and thanked her. As we continued down the street, I couldn't help but wonder what Katina thought about all of this. I suspected she had more than a few questions now: *Why did my mother buy such an expensive gift for a relative she just met? Why haven't I heard of a cousin Maria before now? Does something about Maria seem familiar?* Fortunately, she kept her questions to herself.

Hariklea finished her errands, and we took a taxi home. It was siesta time. As I sat on my bed, I studied my necklace and mused about our strange shopping trip. What could be more ordinary than a mother shopping with her two daughters? Nothing, except one daughter was entirely unaware of the other. When Katina wasn't looking, Hariklea would steal a glance at me, place her hand on her cheek, shake her head, and say, "Poh, Poh, Poh." I think it was the Greek equivalent of "My Oh My" so I smiled and nodded in agreement each time.

One evening Hariklea took us out to dinner at a taverna with tables set just feet from the sea. We chose one near the wooden sidewalk so she wouldn't have to walk in the sand. Taking in the view, I had never seen such a picturesque restaurant. Blue and white checkered tablecloths with vases of yellow daffodils adorned each table. The waiters, in black slacks with white, button-down shirts were attentive to our every desire. The setting sun and the sparkling blue water completed the postcard-perfect scene.

Even in such an idyllic setting, Hariklea was her bossy self. When I ordered two skewers of *souvlaki*, she changed it to three. If I preferred to skip the salad entree, one arrived. When my meal was half-eaten, Hariklea piled more food on my plate without asking and told me I was too thin. As I begged, "Please, no more food," I could barely contain my amusement. Having "bossy" Hariklea take charge and treat me like her daughter was a surprise and filled me with joy. You had to belong to a family to be bossed around by them. Thank you Hariklea!

As the moon reflected off the water like a fiery gem, a cool breeze blew onto the shore. I wiggled my toes into the warm sand to ward off the chill and thought to myself; this must be what dinner is like in heaven.

TIME WITH MAMA

HARIKLEA TOOK TIME OFF WORK, AND IT WASN'T LONG before we settled into a simple daily rhythm. After a light breakfast of fruit and pastry, we cleaned the house, ran errands, and prepared our daily meal. On days spent close to home, I explored Synora, Hariklea's neighborhood. Many of the houses were painted in white or pastel colors with eye-popping doors and shutters. Land was costly, and many of the homes had no space for greenery. So, everything from citrus trees to the vivid bougainvillea that snaked along black iron railings was planted in colorful pots and displayed on balconies.

As I reached the top of the hill, I came upon the neighborhood Kafenion or coffee shop. A low-slung building painted blue and white; it was a home away from home for the men who frequented the place. Small tables with straight-backed wooden chairs and wicker seats sat under a pergola with grape vines woven through the latticework for shade. While the men solved the world's problems, gossiped, or played backgammon, they smoked and sipped strong coffee or *ouzo*, the tradi-tional liquor. These men had perfected the art of relaxation. As I walked past, they stopped everything and stared at me like they'd seen a space alien. I guessed tourists were not a common sight in that neighborhood. As I strolled by an odd thought occurred to me. If I had not been adopted, those men could be friends of mine and wouldn't give me a second look.

One afternoon, Hariklea hired a taxi, and we went sightseeing. We drove around an ancient castle, walked on the waterfront pier, and ate lunch in a quaint taverna near the port. I was acutely aware this city looked and felt different than the first time I had visited. Now I was connected in a way I never thought possible. I had seen Patras through the eyes of a carefree tourist in June but would leave as a daughter and sister in July.

Our travels took us down the street where the orphanage stood. While it was not the same building where I was left, it was still a towering reminder of the worst day of Hariklea's life. Katina was oblivious to its importance, so I kept my eyes on Hariklea. As we passed by, she dropped her head and stared at the floor. Her reaction did not surprise me. Sitting next to the daughter she had left there must have been agonizing. I wanted to reach out and comfort her but knew I could not. I remained silent and waited for my clenched heart to relax.

As we spent time together, I tried to understand Hariklea better. What struck me most was she rarely smiled, much less laughed out loud. I wondered if she had always been like this or had secrets and hardships changed her? During one of our cooking sessions in her small kitchen, I got to see another side of Hariklea. Meal preparation was a challenge as we dodged each other like dancers in a kind of awkward ballet. My job was to slice the *melitzana* (eggplant) for the *moussaka*. I was gathering what I needed for my job when I accidentally hit her in the head with the oven pan. I didn't strike her hard, but Katina and I froze, unsure how she would react. Hariklea paused, gave me a surprised look, and burst into uncontrolled laughter. Katina and I looked at each other and began laughing, too. There we were, the three of us in hysterics until our stomachs hurt. When I regained some self-control, I looked at Hariklea. The tears in her eyes and the delight on her face said it all. For the first time in her life, she had both of her children under one roof, and nothing could spoil her happiness.

Later that day, Hariklea and I were taking a taxi home from the bakery when she did the most disturbing thing. Turning towards me, she made a gun with her hand, placed it to her temple in a shooting motion, and spoke. Alarmed, I asked the driver to translate what she was saying: "She wants to know how you can look at her. She said she gave you away so you should take a gun and shoot her." Those words hit me hard as I realized Hariklea had never forgiven herself for giving me up. Unprepared for her horrible request, I asked the driver to tell Hariklea, "I do not want to kill her. I owe everything, including my life to her." Alas, my gratitude could not alleviate her self-inflicted guilt, and my pleas fell on deaf ears. Her remorse for leaving me at the orphanage ran too deep, and the realization she had missed my childhood tormented her even more. I could only hope the passage of time, and our reconnecting would help heal her wounded soul. Back home, I was thankful it was siesta time. I think we both needed some alone time.

The July heat was intense, even in the evening. With no air conditioning, we tried to stay cool by sipping iced coffees under an olive tree. Katina was pleased when a few relatives stopped by to visit. All was going well until a "real" cousin commented I looked like Hariklea and asked how we were related. Her comment shocked me. *What about me reminded her of Hariklea? Could relatives see similarities others did not? Was I about to be exposed?* I became nervous as all eyes turned on me. Hoping to avoid the conversation, I gave the correct response, "I am Hariklea's cousin on her father's side." There were no more questions, but I could see Hariklea was worried a seed of suspicion had begun to grow. I figured the best way to divert attention from me was to offer to buy ice cream for everyone, so I hastily took orders and headed down the street to escape the questioning stares. Upon my return, the conversation had moved on to other topics, and I could relax.

As I enjoyed my ice cream, I found myself studying Katina. My visit had been a total surprise, yet she had taken everything in stride. Her warm, relaxed manner made her instantly likable. A natural beauty with jet black hair, black eyes, and striking features, she was less than five feet tall. Towering above her at 5'2", I was the family giant. Katina and I did share one thing in common; she didn't look much like Hariklea either. She had her mother's hairline and button nose, but that was all. I was beginning to wonder if we *both* resembled our fathers.

I had been in Hariklea's home for a week, and my time in Greece was coming to an end. I was packed and ready to go but had one important stop to make before I returned to the States. A taxi would arrive shortly to take me to the bus station. From there I was riding a bus south to the town of Gastouni and taking a cab for the short distance to the Ionian Village. I had checked the travel schedule and knew they would be at the camp. This incredible adventure had started with Father George just a few weeks ago, and I needed to thank him for introducing me to Father Paul and Evi. Most of all, I wanted to see his face when I told him whom we had found.

My taxi pulled up, and it was time to go. The three of us walked outside, and Katina and I started crying right away. I hugged and kissed her like family in anticipation of the day she learned I was her sister. We promised to write letters, and I pledged to return as often as possible. We slowly parted, and I turned my attention to Hariklea. Saying goodbye to her would be difficult. We held each other and wept; not only for the joy in finding one another but for the time we had missed together. I told the driver I was his only passenger, but I needed his help to translate something private for Hariklea. He consented and hopped in the front seat while she and I got in the back. My question to Hariklea before I left was just: "Are you happy or sad I found you?"

With a wry smile, Hariklea replied, "I am both. I am happy because I always knew I had a daughter in America, and you found me. But I am also sad because now I have one more person to worry about!" I laughed out loud and hugged her. It was the perfect thing for a Mother to say.

HIS EMINENCE

CLIMBING ABOARD, I LOOKED FORWARD TO THE SOLITUDE provided by the bus ride to Gastouni. The steady hum of the bus engine helped me relax as I closed my eyes and savored the recent memories. After three decades apart, I had found my birth mother in two days. Two days! I could scarcely believe it still. Asking me to stay in her home was a wise and loving gesture from Hariklea. It allowed all three of us to get acquainted as a family and begin the healing process. It meant the world to Hariklea to have both daughters home with her. And Katina and I each got the sister we'd always wanted.

From Gastouni, I grabbed a taxi to the Ionian Village where the high school session was in full swing. Counselors and teenagers were everywhere, enjoying a free afternoon at the camp. Unaware I was coming; I surprised Father George when I found him at a table in the dining area. It was delightful to see him again as we greeted each other like old friends. His face lit up when I told him I'd returned to share some big news with him. Father's evening schedule was full of camp activities, so he offered me an empty cottage where I could spend the night. We agreed to meet at his office the next morning.

Up early, I headed straight for Father George's office. As I approached, I saw a high-ranking Orthodox priest sitting near the office door reading a book. His hair and long beard were snow white, and he wore a round black hat with a flat top on his head. A black veil flowed down past his shoulders, and the stark black cassock (ankle-length robe) accentuated the exquisite cross hanging around his neck. I wished him a "good morning" and entered the office.

Before I even sat down, I proclaimed, "I found my birth mother!" Father George was in disbelief when I told him how quickly and dramatically, Father Paul, Evi and I had found Hariklea Voukelatos. I shared her remarkable story: from her exile to Patras while seven months pregnant, to the crushing guilt she still carried over losing me, to the healing moments in her home.

"How do you I feel about all this, Maria," he asked.

I shook my head as I replied, "I'm still reeling from the events of this past week. It's not easy to change truths I have believed my entire life. It was a huge shock to find them untrue. My only expectation had been to explore Patras and find the location of the orphanage. Everything changed when I learned it was still there. Now thanks to you, Father Paul and Evi, I found my birth mother and a half-sister."

"You have not been alone on this journey, Maria. I see evidence of God's grace at every turn in your story," replied Father George.

"Yes, I know I am very blessed."

Our conversation was winding down when I remembered my baptism certificate. Despite Father Paul's efforts, I had resigned myself to the possibility I might never find it. It was not at the City Hall, the orphanage, or the hospital, and once I was back in the U.S., it would be nearly impossible to obtain it. I asked Father George for a suggestion.

His face brightened as he answered, "Just a moment, I know someone who might be able to help you."

He opened his office door and asked the priest to come inside. Father George introduced me to His Eminence, Gabriel, one of 12 Bishops who sat on the Holy Synod in Istanbul, Turkey. No ordinary priest, he answered directly to the Patriarch, the leader of the Orthodox Christian world, a man equal to the Pope in status. Fluent in five languages, His Eminence had accepted an invitation by the Greek government to visit the Ionian Village, and he was leaving this very morning. Father George asked me to share my adoption story and then inquire about my baptism paper. I gave His Eminence an abbreviated version and asked my question.

You could have knocked me over with a feather when he answered, "I was once an orphan too, and I would like to help. The Metropolitan of Patras (who oversees all Greek churches in southern Greece), is a friend of mine. I will go to his office in Saint Andrew's Cathedral with you and speak to him on your behalf." I was touched by his generous offer but did not understand how he was going to accomplish this. I told him I had reached the I.V. by bus and taxi. He told me he'd arrived in a Mercedes Benz with a driver. *We didn't travel in the same circles.* His Eminence cleared things up when he told me we would be taking a public bus to Patras together. His driver would take us as far as the bus station and then go on ahead to Saint Andrews in Patras. Father George and I exchanged confused glances. A public bus, was he kidding?

His Eminence was serious because 45 minutes later, I was sitting in the back of a spacious Mercedes on soft leather seats that felt like warm butter against my bare skin. Now, this was the way to travel! Too bad, we were only going a few miles. I knew that to avoid even the appearance of impropriety, His Eminence could not be seen riding in a car alone for three hours with a young woman.

All too soon we arrived at the bus station. I was a nervous wreck as I followed His Eminence into the dingy building. I didn't want to do or say the least thing wrong or inappropriate. Despite my protests, he bought two bus tickets and two Cokes. We found a small round metal table with matching chairs, sat and waited. As I sipped my coke and took in the surroundings, I hid the smile on my face as a genuinely American thought came to mind: *This would make one hell of a Coca Cola commercial!*

As travelers entered the bus station and spied His Eminence, their behavior changed. No ordinary priest, their first reaction was shock followed by the sound of dropping luggage. They couldn't bow low enough or cross themselves fast enough when they saw him. It was impressive, but I was more nervous than ever now. On the bus, I cautiously took the seat next to him, unsure of the protocol for a man of his station. He seemed fine with it, so I sat down and tried to relax as we headed for Patras.

Passing through small towns, the riders we picked up along the way were as startled as the passengers in Gastouni. People boarded the bus and shook their heads in disbelief when they saw us. Trying to find their seat while they carried bags, bowed, and crossed themselves was no easy task. The locals could not fathom His Eminence taking a bus anywhere, much less accompanying a woman wearing shorts and a tank top. I felt honored to be traveling with such an esteemed man who took all the fuss in stride.

In hindsight, my fears of saying or doing something incorrect were foolish. His Eminence had a warmth to him that belied his formal position. He was well-traveled, knowledgeable, and he laughed easily. We discussed everything from the I.V. and world affairs to basketball, his favorite sport. Engrossed in our conversation, I didn't even notice when the bus stopped in front of Saint Andrew's. We exited the bus and stood on the sidewalk as it pulled away.

Facing the cathedral, His Eminence looked at my clothes and wagged his finger. I would have to wait outside while he met with the Metropolitan. As I watched him enter the towering church, I could have kicked myself for not changing into appropriate clothes before we left this morning. It would have been such a privilege to attend a meeting between those two priests. Forced to sit outside, I found a wall and waited.

His Eminence returned 20 minutes later and announced, "I have good news. The priest who baptized you served his parish for 50 years and is still alive. The Metropolitan will contact him, and he will issue you a new baptismal certificate. Since you are leaving for home tomorrow, I asked him to send the new document to the orphanage where your friends can pick it up and mail it to you in America."

As if on cue, the Mercedes pulled up to take His Eminence to Athens for his evening flight back to Turkey. I thanked him profusely for going out of his way to help a former orphan. As he got in the car, he handed me his card and added, "Call me in Turkey if you have any problems." In an instant, he was gone, leaving me dumbstruck, waving good-bye, and scarcely believing what had just happened.

Like His Eminence, I was going home too. I was going to catch a bus to Athens for my early morning flight to the States. It was a perfect way for my Greek odyssey to end.

TELLING ELLEN/TELLING MOM

LIFE BACK HOME WAS A WHIRLWIND OF ACTIVITY AS I busied myself with finding a teaching job. I did not want to substitute teach for another year. In early August, when a principal called me to interview for a sixth-grade position, I wore the necklace Hariklea had bought me in Patras for luck. It was a superstitious thing to do, but I got the job. With my employment needs met, I made plans to visit Ellen, my adoptive mother, in San Diego before school started. Mom and I had talked on the phone since my return, but I had kept the conversation light with the promise she would see and hear everything when I got to town.

Among friends, reactions to my story were similar; there was wide-eyed shock followed by disbelief. When they examined the photographs of Hariklea, their reaction mirrored the Greeks. Everyone had an opinion on whether we looked alike. By the end of my tale, tears were flowing, and someone would comment, "Your story should be a movie!" One friend, I never learned who, called the local newspaper, and a reporter interviewed me in my home. When the article came out, I enjoyed my one minute of fame.

I was happy my story had touched people so profoundly, but there was one person I worried about telling, Mom. Dad had passed away the year before, and she was alone after 43 years of marriage. I did not want to add to her pain. Having to tell my adoptive mother, I had found my birth mother was a scenario I could never have imagined. Ellen had wanted a child so badly I didn't want her to think I was ungrateful, disloyal, or she was losing me to my *real* Mom. Ellen was the most selfless person I knew, and I loved her more than anyone in the world. She had adopted and loved me unconditionally, and I would take this secret to my grave rather than hurt her. Fortunately, I still had a little time to decide.

One day I came home to find a letter from Katina. Covered with beautiful, ornate, stamps, I almost ruined them as I tore open the envelope. Thankfully the letter was written in simple English. Katina told me two weeks after I left, Hariklea had told her the truth about me. She was not upset with her mother. Katina understood her mother's hesitation to share the existence of another child but finding a sister was an unexpected revelation for her. She was overjoyed, and I was relieved I had not caused a problem between the two. Now the "cousin from America" story could be officially retired, and I could spend candid time with my Greek family.

The rest of August flew by as I spent countless hours getting my first classroom ready for the September start date. I had 26 kids on my roster and couldn't wait to meet them. My San Diego plans were also complete. The only thing left was to put my photographs into an album. Unlike Mom, who was motivated by love when she selected my album years before, my motivation was fear as I chose one with easily removable pages. I was still undecided on what to tell Mom, so it gave me options.

Upon arrival, I picked up my car and headed to Mom's home in San Diego's backcountry. The baseball-sized knot in my stomach was a constant reminder of what lay ahead. I tried to ease my apprehension with thoughts of how receptive Mom had been about adoption – not just mine, but my three siblings as well. She had spent countless hours making scrapbooks filled with their adoption artifacts too. Richard Jr. and Deirdre's albums even included their mother's name.

In the past month, I had found a mother and a sister, discoveries I was still processing. I was excited to know my new family, but I wanted to protect the one I had. It was a delicate balance I struggled to maintain. My fears of hurting Mom took on a life of their own and nearly blinded me from believing she could accept such a truth. With her house in sight, the knot in my stomach was now the size of a basketball. I pulled off the road and gathered myself before I continued. Mom knew I was on the way, so there was no turning back. With no guidebook on how to handle this type of situation, I had only one choice. Face the music and trust the Mother who loved and raised me.

Pulling into her driveway, Mom came outside to greet me, and I hugged her a little longer than usual. Her arms around me felt like home; safe and familiar. In the kitchen, my senses were delighted by the delicious aromas of my favorite meal, baked chicken, carrot-raisin salad, and chocolate cake made from scratch. As I fawned over the food she had prepared, we caught up on family news. Brother Michael was working as an RN in a San Diego hospital, and the twins were in the wind – God only knew where.

I was putting my luggage in the spare room when Mom came to the door and asked a question that stopped me cold. "So, did you meet any relatives while you were over there?"

I busied myself with my suitcase, and after a long pause, I managed a weak, "Yes."

Her next question was the one I dreaded: "Who did you find?"

My throat constricted and I could barely speak, so I deflected with a question of my own. "Mom, guess the most unbelievable relative you can imagine?"

"You found your mother, didn't you?"

I mumbled, "Yes."

"Oh my God, you found your mother? I want to hear all about it," Mom proclaimed.

Stunned, I stood there like a statue, unable to move or speak. The weeks of angst had been for naught, and my fear of hurting Ellen had consumed me unnecessarily. Mom's questions made this more comfortable than I could have dreamed. Relaxing a bit, I wondered what had prompted her initial question. Had Mom suspected I was hiding something during our telephone conversations? Could she sense I was carrying an emotional burden? I knew it was now or never, so I went to the bedroom, grabbed the album, and set it on the kitchen table. I patted the chair next to me, invited Mom to sit, and began.

The photos were invaluable as I led Mom through my two months in Greece. I started with pictures from my I.V. days and ended with my time in Patras. I moved through them at a deliberate pace, hoping we wouldn't spend too much time on the pictures of Hariklea. As we neared the photographs of her, my fears returned, and I was overwhelmed by feelings of betrayal. I looked away and questioned my decision as Mom examined the woman who had given birth to "her" child. *I hope Mom doesn't think I look like Hariklea. Should I have included the photos with my arm around her? What about the pictures of Hariklea, Katina and me, arm in arm at the taverna?*

"She looks like a nice woman. What's her name?" was all Mom asked.

"Her name is Hariklea, and she is nice. The young woman is her daughter, Katina."

Mom was surprised Patras still had an orphanage with such good records, but she was bowled over when I described how we found Hariklea. I didn't know much yet, but I shared what she had told me about her life. When I told Mom I had spent a week in Hariklea's home with Katina, she was happy for me and wanted details of our time together. Mom couldn't imagine dining by the sea with your feet in the sand, but she laughed when I shared stories of Hariklea's bossy personality. I concluded with a comment about her generosity but did not mention the soul-crushing guilt she still felt over losing me. Mom didn't need to hear that.

We finished looking at the album and enjoyed the meal she had prepared. After we washed the dishes, I went for a walk along the stream running by her house. I knew Mom needed some private time with her thoughts and the photo album. I was gone for a half-hour but returned to the back of the house so I could peek through a window and see if she was finished. There she was sitting at the table, hunched over the album and staring at *the* page. I knew which photos Mom was glued to, and I couldn't imagine how she felt right now. *Did she feel threatened by my birth mother? Was this the day Mom feared might come? Would she worry I loved her any less?* I felt happy, sad, and vulnerable as I watched her study, the photographs of Hariklea. Tears sprung from my eyes and ran down my cheeks as I quietly watched her. I wanted to give Mom all the time she needed, so I went for another walk. The second time around, I made a noisy entrance via the front door to announce my arrival.

TALKING LIKE FAMILY

AFTER FINDING MY FAMILY IN 1984, I TRAVELED TO GREECE as often as my finances would allow. I felt an urgency about my trips like I needed to make up for the lost time. Plane tickets to Greece were quite expensive, so I needed a plan if I wanted to travel on a teacher's salary. I volunteered for every district committee I could and kept two nights a week waiting tables at the restaurant.

Over the next years, my Greek family saw significant changes. Sister Katina married George, an accountant who worked at the Post Office. His personality resembled Hariklea's. He was an introvert who rarely smiled, but he was a quietly supportive husband. The small house was impossible for three people to live in, so Hariklea built a new home. Near the center of Patras, the house rose two stories, boasted 8' ceilings, ceramic tile floors, and soft pastel colors. There was new furniture in the living room and all three bedrooms. The kitchen sported new appliances and opened into a formal dining room. A balcony filled with potted plants completed the lovely home.

Since Hariklea had paid for the new construction, I doubt there was much discussion about the living arrangements. She knew a young couple needed their own space, so Hariklea wisely designed the home with an apartment of her own. I had no idea how she paid for it. Maybe she was good at saving her salary, or Vasilis, her late husband, had left her some money. I guessed both might have been true, but felt it was indiscreet to ask.

Katina and George settled into the spacious home and started a family. Two sons, Christos and Vasilis, were born three years apart. Christos inherited Katina's dark features and was a live wire who shrieked at the top of his lungs and danced on a whim. Vasilis had George's lighter features but was more introspective. He loved reading, drawing, and following Christos around.

Hariklea's legacy to Katina was a new home. Her legacy to me would be the details of her life. Katina knew the truth about me now, so I felt free to ask almost anything. I took careful notes on their answers and returned with new questions on each visit. These were the times when the three of us shared funny, poignant, moments as we grew to trust each other like family.

One day out of the blue, Katina looked at me and exclaimed, "Maria, you biiiiiig wooooman!" Being the tallest at 5'2" and the largest, this was a first for me. Both Hariklea and my sister were well under 5' tall and Katina weighed barely 100 lbs. The difference in our sizes was considerable, which prompted me to ask Hariklea if she would answer questions about her genetic history. Until that day, I had never made such an inquiry, but it felt good. I didn't care if I got a partial account, at least I would get *some* answers.

To my relief, Hariklea told me there were no inherited diseases on her side of the family, only a predisposition toward anemia. Katina's children had taken liquid iron for anemia since they were babies, and I suffered from the same condition. Every six months or so I'd go the doctor, get blood drawn, and wait for the results. If I was anemic, I would supplement my diet with iron pills. Finding the link to my anemia gave me a better understanding of inherited medical maladies, but more importantly; it gave me someone to blame.

Next, I wanted to find out who was responsible for the spider-veins that made a road map of my legs and back. Growing up in San Diego where shorts were in year-round, my "old lady legs" had been an embarrassment since middle school. Some of my veins had even grouped to form clusters, one of which was a dead ringer for the contours of Australia. I hated them. When I examined Hariklea and Katina, both were spider vein free. I was surprised and irritated, but Hariklea brought down the house when she joked, "Those must have come from your father's side."

Other than the rape, Hariklea had never mentioned my father, Yiorgos. *Was this a sign I could ask the question I had avoided for years? Would she reveal anything about the man who hurt her so deeply?* I decided to risk it and asked Hariklea to tell me about Yiorgos. Her answer was brief, "He was an olive grower, the village carpenter, and a handyman. He was beautiful, but he was a bad man." It wasn't much of an answer, so I let it go. Hariklea was still not ready to discuss him. We could revisit the subject another day.

Sitting on the sofa one morning, the three of us rested our legs on the coffee table and compared our feet. At size 7.0, my feet were the largest. Hariklea's were next at size 6.0, followed by Katina's at 5.0. This exercise only added to my "biiiiiig wooooman" image. The foot inspections ended with Katina and me giggling like schoolgirls when we discovered we had identical toes.

I knew Greeks often named their children after the children's grandparents, so I asked Hariklea how she selected my name. She told me I was baptized in the hospital chapel, Saint Charalambos ten days after I was born and given the name "Maria" for protection. Unsure of her future Hariklea felt sharing a name with the Virgin Mary would protect me and help secure my survival.

One visit, Hariklea asked me about my family in America so the next summer I brought a photograph of them to Greece. Dad hated having his picture taken, so the photo I brought was of Mom and the four kids. While I packed for this trip, I sadly realized I did not own a photograph of all six Paces together. I watched her study the picture of my family and thought about Mom doing the same thing with Hariklea's photo. Both women knew about each other, but now they had a face to go with the name. Hariklea took a long look at the photo and responded with a few questions. "Is this your mother? Who are these other children? If she already had three children, why did she need to adopt you?"

I smiled, pointed to the picture, and explained, "Yes, that is my mother; her name is Ellen. All these children were orphans like me. My brother and I were adopted from Greek orphanages, and the twins were given up by a young unwed mother in San Diego. Ellen is a good woman who gave four orphaned children a home Hariklea." Her demeanor softened as she processed what I had said. Perhaps she also pondered how I had just spoken up for my adoptive mother, calling her unequivocally "a good woman." Hariklea responded she was grateful I was well cared for, and I sensed she had gained a new respect for Ellen.

Mealtime was always an anxious time for me, whether in Greece or America, because I was a finicky eater. Mealtime was stressful enough without the burden of disliking feta cheese, tomatoes or olives; staples of the Greek diet. If I had a dollar for every time someone asked me, "How can you be Greek and not like olives, tomatoes, and feta?" I would be rich! As a child, I was expected to eat all the food on my plate because there were "starving children in Africa." That's when large napkins, Formica tables with hollow legs, and large pockets came in handy. I had no idea why I disliked those foods, but as I sat across from Hariklea, I asked her for an explanation. Her response was terse but telling. She shrugged her shoulders, forced a smile, and declared, "I didn't raise you." Sadly, not even her wry smile could hide the pain in her eyes as she tried to make a joke.

The years passed by and Hariklea revealed her story to me in bits and pieces. My detailed notes helped me put together the how's and why's that weigh on so many adoptees. *How did I come to be? What happened to my mother that left her with no other option than to place me in an orphanage? Why didn't she come back for me?* I don't have all the pieces to this puzzle that arrived with no picture to guide me, but I found the box they came in. It is Hariklea's story as she told me.

TAKE THE FORK IN THE ROAD

TRAVELING WITH BEV, A FRIEND, AND FELLOW TEACHER, we arrived on the island of Lefkada, Greece on July 1st, 1996, exactly 40 years to the day after I had arrived in San Diego. We did not plan it that way, but it was the first of many "coincidences" we would witness that week. The only thing I knew about Lefkada fit into one, sad, locked door sentence – Hariklea's father disowned her and forced her into exile in Patras, and she had not seen her village since. When I had asked Hariklea the name of her town, her reply puzzled me. "I don't know. I think it started with an 'N,' but I don't think it's even there anymore," was all she said. Hariklea wasn't sure where she grew up? I didn't believe that for a minute. She remembered, but it hurt me to see how fiercely after all these years she still guarded her secrets.

Hariklea's response back then planted the seed of visiting Lefkada. Her childhood was a piece of the puzzle I did not have, the final piece. I hoped she would not see my search for her village as an intrusion. On this trip to see Hariklea, I held the secrets. I did not tell her I was going to Lefkada *before* I visited her in Patras and had to admit I was a little worried about how she would react. I didn't want to damage the close relationship I enjoyed with my Patras family. I was merely trying to fill in some of my blanks and complete the story of *me*.

Ten years after finding Hariklea, Bev and I drove past the drawbridge and over the causeway onto Lefkada Island. The drive was exhausting, so we stopped at the Hotel Lefkas, the first one we saw. Our room had a view of the boat-filled harbor and promenade crowded with restaurants and shops. We relaxed awhile then set out to explore Lefkas town, the capital and largest city on the island. With every building painted a different pastel color, the entire place oozed Greek charm. The unique architecture was the town's most distinct feature: all the second story walls and church steeples were designed using rare techniques of earthquake proofing. The second story walls were constructed using corrugated metal, and the church steeples' steel latticework looked like Greek versions of the Eiffel tower.

A morning stroll into town for crepes and coffee became a daily ritual before we hopped in the car for a day of sightseeing and exploring. We chose Lefkada because it was Hariklea's island, but there were other reasons: You didn't need a ferry ride to get there. It was home to Porto Katziki, one of the most spectacular beaches in the world. Vasiliki, a town at the southern end of the island was the windsurfing capital of Europe. While not as quaint as Lefkas, it prided itself on excellent restaurants, hotels, and big wind that arrived every day at precisely 3:00 p.m. We spent our days sunning on white sand beaches, dining on fresh calamari, and shopping for folk art in villages with names like Hortata and Karya.

Towards the end of the week, Bev and I took a tourist break and decided to find Hariklea's village. Looking back, I asked myself why I had waited so many days to begin looking. On a subconscious level, had I delayed the search? Was I afraid I wouldn't find her village or was

I worried I would? Those were valid questions worth considering, but I didn't have any answers.

As we left the hotel, I asked the manager if he knew the name Voukelatos. He told us there were several people named Voukelatos on Lefkada; it was a common name. When I asked about villages that began with "N," he told us about Agios Nikolaos, located at the southern end of the island. He wasn't sure it still existed. I remembered Hariklea told me there was a possibility no one lived in her village. Undeterred, we decided playing detective would be a fun way to spend the day, so we headed south.

We questioned people at every church, village, or town that began with an "N" with no luck. In the hills just above Vasiliki, we came to a fork in the road. There was a sign with the names of two villages on it, Manassi to the left and Nikolis to the right. I turned to Bev and pointed, "Well, the one on the right begins with an 'N,' let's go see what's there." Just past the sign pointing to Nikolis, we found ourselves heading down a steep hill with a sweeping view of the valley to the Mediterranean. A white-washed market advertising cold drinks was a welcome sight. Hot and thirsty, we parked in the shade and entered. Under a twisted olive tree guarding the store sat five men around a table enjoying the summer day. Four older men had silver-streaked black hair, dark eyes, and leather-like faces that had spent a lifetime under the Mediterranean sun. The young man looked to be in his late teens with loose sand-colored curls, brown eyes, and a fair complexion.

We were leaving the shop when almost on a whim, I asked the group under the tree if anyone spoke English. The young man replied, "I do."

Relieved, I asked him if he would answer some questions for me. He agreed, so I repeated the question I had asked so many times that day. "Do you know the name, Voukelatos?"

"Yes, I am a Voukelatos," he responded. I was surprised but remembered the hotel manager had told me there were many Greeks with that name on the island. I continued and asked if he knew a Zoe or Efstathios Voukelatos.

Pointing, he said in perfect English, "Those are my grandparents' names, and they are buried right over there." I looked across the street and saw an old cemetery with long-neglected marble headstones.

I continued, "Those are *my* grandparents' names, too. Do you know if they had three sons, Nikos, Dimitris, and Thodoris?"

Warily he replied, "Yes. Nikos is my father and Thodoris is my uncle. Our families share the house they built in the village. Another uncle, Dimitris, lives in Athens."

I was astounded; I had found Hariklea's village! With my heart hammering in my chest, I spread my arms apart to emphasize the enormity of my next question, "Did they also have a daughter named Hariklea?"

The young man stood up and stared at me with wide-eyed disbelief. "Yes, she is my aunt, but I have never met her. I was raised to think poorly of her because she brought shame to our family, but as an adult, I realized what happened was not her fault."

"Hariklea is my mother," I whispered.

The young man looked like he had just seen a ghost as he cried out, "I am your cousin, Stathis, and everyone thinks you are dead!"

Behind me, I could hear Bev repeating, "No way, no way. This is not happening again!"

Stathis ran to me, and we collapsed into one another's arms, both in disbelief over what had just happened. When we were finally able to speak, we all walked up the road and found a quiet place to talk. Time with Stathis was like meeting someone I had known my entire life – we had an instant connection. He was warm and kind and wore his heart on his sleeve. His English skills were a blessing as I told him what I knew about Hariklea; from the tragedy in Nikolis to losing me through a foreign adoption program in Patras.

We continued to talk as Stathis gave us a tour of his village. The school, he and his brothers, attended had one-room. The church was ample for such a small town and looked like it had been remodeled. Entering the nearby cemetery, I was surprised to find the entire grave-yard filled with Voukelatoses dating back to the 1800s. I was related to everyone buried there! It didn't take me long to locate my grandpar-ents' graves. Zoe and Efstathios were buried side by side under a white marble headstone shaped like a cross. The quiet grave site belied the awful reality of their lives together. Only in death had they found peace.

We finished the tour and were heading back to our car when Stathis asked, "Do you want to meet your uncles, Nikos and Thodoris? Our home is very close."

My response was immediate: "No, I don't think that would be a good idea. Everyone thinks I am dead, and we should leave it that way. No one is going to be happy to see me."

Stathis did not give up, "Well, you're not leaving. My family has suffered more than 40 years because of something that was not Hariklea's fault. Times have changed, and the heartache needs to end right now. Let's go; it's time to meet your uncles!"

We followed Stathis down a steep dirt path to the heart of Nikolis where houses were jumbled and tucked into the nooks and crannies of the jagged hillside. Two hours earlier, I didn't know anyone on Lefkada. Now I was on my way to meet two uncles with the cousin I had just met! Soon we were standing in front of a white-washed two-story home with a large flagstone patio and an arbor heavy with fruit and garlic braids. Under the arbor were four straight-backed wooden chairs and a simple table for dining. Flowers of every color formed a cheerful perimeter around the patio. Rolls of black plastic netting sat under olive trees for the fall harvest. Cicadas screeched from their lofty perches. The warm Greek sun and the salty sea air completed the magic of the scene.

Stathis motioned for us to sit at the table as two women approached. Both were wearing simple, button-up, cotton dresses, and tired sandals. Zahareena, Stathis' mother, was the more outgoing of the two. Short and stout with black hair and brown skin, she was married to Nikos, Hariklea's youngest brother. Marianna, his aunt, was taller, with blue eyes and a fair complexion. She was married to Hariklea's older brother, Thodoris.

"What are you going to tell your family about us?" I asked.

"When my sister and I were in school, we were always bringing friends home; I'm going to tell them you are school friends."

I chuckled as I imagined this handsome 18-year-old trying to pass off two older women as school friends. Stathis made the introductions, but the women's confused responses exposed their skepticism. I don't think Zahareena and Marianna believed the "school friends" story for even a moment. They had no idea who I was, but I looked forward to their reaction when they learned I was their niece.

While we waited for the men to return home for lunch, the wives served us an odd-looking treat. In a tall glass of cold water, sat a teaspoon loaded with a sticky substance that looked like Elmer's glue. Bev and I had no idea what to do, so I asked Stathis to explain, "It's called a "spoon sweet" because the serving size is a full teaspoon. It was offered to guests in ancient times as a symbol of hospitality. There are many different kinds, and we make ours with sweet vanilla crème. You're supposed to lick the cream like a lollipop, stick it back in the glass of water, and repeat until the cream is gone." The "spoon sweet" proved to be quite tasty and a way to keep my hands busy while we waited for my uncles.

The views of the sun-splashed valley and the bright blue Ionian Sea filled with windsurfers did little to ease my nerves. I was still worried about Stathis' decision. He was a young man whose thinking expressed the changing times, but the village elders might not feel the same. The last thing I wanted to do was cause more pain to a family that had seen more than its share of tragedy. After 20 minutes, two men approached from down the hill. Both men had fit bodies from the many years of manual labor, full heads of thick, silver, hair, and bronzed skin. They looked puzzled when they saw us and were asked to sit down at the table. Their wives tiptoed away and observed us from the kitchen doorway.

Stathis murmured to me, "I'm going to tell them now."

I sorely regretted my lack of fluent Greek as I listened to him quietly tell his father and uncle the news that would change their lives. When he finished, Nikos turned away and stared out across the valley. Thodoris dropped his head and began twisting his gold watch round and round his wrist. They had not seen their sister since she was 15, and both believed her baby had died. I could not imagine all the feelings news of my existence had stirred up. The shock must have been traumatic, especially for Thodoris. Abruptly, he got up from the table and left. When I asked where he was going, Stathis softly stated, "He is going to cry."

Bev, Uncle Nikos, my aunts, Stathis, and I sat there in uneasy silence. I noticed Nikos would steal glances at me and then look away. I avoided direct eye contact so he wouldn't feel uncomfortable. His comment, I had Hariklea's eyes, shocked me. Did Nikos believe I was his niece? I wasn't sure. An hour later, with tear-stained cheeks and a heart-broken expression, Thodoris returned to the table and sat in silence. Meanwhile, Stathis had sunk lower and lower in his chair while Bev and I furtively tried to figure out what to do.

When he admitted, "Maybe this wasn't a good idea after all. I may have hurt them," I asked if we should leave.

Stathis translated my comment to Thodoris, who responded loudly and angrily, "Don't be silly, this was not your fault."

I wasn't sure what he meant, but more silence followed his response. We continued to sit around the table while Zahareena and Mariana served a traditional Greek lunch of chicken, salad, and bread. I was happy for the distraction when they urged us to eat. Sitting next to Thodoris, I had seen enough to know there was a tender heart underneath his rough exterior. I decided to test his sense of humor and avoid eating the salad tomatoes, anything to break the tension. I ate a few cucumbers and waited for an opening to flip a red beauty onto Thodoris' plate. I waited a few minutes and flipped another one. Soon, a cucumber flew onto my plate, followed by the barest hint of a smile. We continued flipping vegetables until I had all the cucumber slices and Thodoris had all the tomatoes. A picky eater, I didn't need to speak to communicate my food preferences! As we enjoyed our meal, my thoughts turned to Hariklea. She should not be in Patras, but right here, enjoying this special occasion with her family.

As lunch ended, I asked Stathis about taking a photograph. He translated my request, and they began to gather in a group. Still a bit fearful of his reaction, I went to stand by Thodoris. As I approached, he looked in my eyes and reached out his hand. The first thing he grabbed was my thumb. Then, entwining his fingers with mine, he pulled me into him and held on tightly. We held each other close as everyone breathed a sigh of relief and cheered. Thodoris became the patriarch of the family after his father died, and his acceptance of me was a defining moment for the entire family. Love filled his face as he released me and accepted the child; he thought was dead. Nikos, Zahareena, and Marianna who had waited to see what Thodoris would do, hurried over and smothered me with hugs and kisses.

We eventually managed to take a few photos, but the long emotional day had taken its toll. Bev and I needed to drive down the hill to Vasiliki and get a room for the night. Stathis was going to show us the nightlife, and we needed some rest. Tomorrow we would be returning to Nikolis for a family lunch and meet his sister, Eve, who would be home from college.

Bev was exhausted and turned in early, so it was just Stathis and me out on the town in Vasiliki. Over drinks at his favorite haunt, I asked him how he had told his father and uncle about me. "I told them, this may shock you, but this is your niece. She is Hariklea's daughter; her name is Maria."

Stathis added, "After you left, the family discussed at length what had happened, and everyone was *very* okay with all of this." He went on to share an interesting tidbit that added to the magic of the day. While getting ready for work, he had listened to his horoscope on the TV and heard, "something unexpected would occur today." After meeting me, I wondered if he would ever miss his horoscope again.

Later that evening, Stathis and I headed to the beach where we sat for hours sharing everything from family stories to political and cultural issues in our countries. We could hardly believe the chances of meeting under the olive tree. Stathis spent summer nights in Vasiliki waiting tables, chasing girls, and sleeping in the small house his family owned. He was rarely in Nikolis, let alone sitting under an olive tree by the side of the road. It was a miracle as if he had been waiting for us. Stathis' insistence I stay and meet my uncles revealed maturity and wisdom far beyond his years. Without him taking the lead, I might never have met my aunts and uncles, seen my mother's village, or learned about the rest of my extended family.

A MONARCH VISITS

THE NEXT DAY, WHILE DRIVING THE NARROW ROADS BACK to Nikolis, we passed a man sitting sideways on a donkey carrying a bundle of greenery. Both he and the donkey looked hot and thirsty as they slowly made their way up the steep hill. It was a postcard image if I ever saw one. I did a double take when I realized it was my uncle Nikos going home for lunch.

Arriving in Nikolis, we met Stathis' sister, Eve. She had dark shoulder length hair, brown eyes, and fair skin like her brother. Eve had heard the news of how Hariklea's daughter had found Stathis and her family. When she saw me, she began yelling, "my cousin, my cousin" and smothered me with hugs and kisses. Fluent in English, funny and smart, I liked Eve instantly.

Turning to the table, I was humbled by the care my aunts had taken with the meal. Under the shade of the arbor stood a table covered with a colorful, hand-embroidered tablecloth. There were steaming dishes filled with *potatoes* and *keftedes* (meatballs). Deep olive wood bowls overflowed with salad and homemade bread. The smells of garlic, oregano, lemon juice, and bread made my stomach growl with anticipation. Emotions poured over me in a torrent as I sat in Hariklea's mountain village about to enjoy a meal with my two uncles, two aunts, and two cousins. To a person, my family had welcomed me unconditionally. I loved them already, and it frightened me to think what I might have missed if Bev and I had taken the left fork in the road.

Before we started eating, Stathis went inside the house and brought out a jug of homemade *krasi* and eight crystal wine glasses. He poured everyone a drink before he spoke, "Welcome home, Maria. Nikolis is your village and you are related to everyone here. Today is an important day for all of us." With that, my family raised their glasses and toasted the return of their long-lost relative. I was so overcome by the magnitude and the tenderness of the moment it took all my strength not to break down and sob. It touched me to the depths of my soul. I had found Hariklea's family – my family and, in a way, my home.

Everyone took a moment to compose themselves as we began to pass the food. Cousin Eve was just about to reach for the salad when something strange happened. A beautiful monarch butterfly flew slowly across the table and lit upon a cucumber. Its brilliant orange and black wings gently opened and closed. I thought nothing of it, but everyone around the table stopped moving and stared as if in a trance. The longer the monarch remained perched on the cucumber slice, the more unsettled they became. It was as if time had stopped and the air had been sucked out of Nikolis. I looked at Stathis. He explained a monarch butterfly could represent two things to Greeks: a dead relative is trying to contact a living one, or it is a sign from God. "Maybe your grandmother, Zoe, is welcoming you home, or it's a sign God's hand is in this," he observed.

I sat quietly for a moment. I had heard a miracle defined as an event that renders God's hand visible. Finding Hariklea and Stathis was evidence a higher power was at work here. I believed God *and* Zoe were welcoming me home.

After a life-changing week on Lefkada, Bev and I drove to Patras to visit Hariklea. I waited until we got settled and were enjoying cold drinks on the balcony before I told her we had visited Lefkada and found Nikolis. When she heard my news, she was surprised but not upset with me. I think she may have even felt a bit relieved. Hariklea understood my desire to connect with the rest of my family, and I think she wanted the same connection for herself.

I don't know who made the first move, but after finding my Nikolis family, communication between Hariklea and her brothers was reestablished with phone calls and later with visits. As the brothers had reason to pass through Patras, they made sure to visit their sister in the city. When Thodoris her closest brother, needed heart surgery in Athens, he and Marianna broke up the long trip by spending the night in Patras with Hariklea.

I was not there for what Katina described as a small window into her mother's painful past and one of the most touching scenes she had ever witnessed. When Thodoris saw Hariklea for the first time in more than 40 years, it was as if a dam had burst. Tears flowed out in a torrent as he held his sister close, kissed her face, and whispered in her ear. When they were too exhausted to stand, they moved to the couch, still holding onto each other. Thodoris wept for joy, but he also shed bitter tears of self-recrimination for the way Hariklea was treated.

At the time, Thodoris had not understood the real reason behind his sister's exile, and he supported his father's decision. He had been torn between his obligation to protect the family honor, duty to his father, and love for the sister he could not protect. When he learned the truth about what happened, his guilt became almost too much to bear. Their tears slowed to a trickle as they sat together for hours holding hands and healing their hearts. I would have loved to share such a moment with my sister.

The week Bev and I spent on Lefkada was dreamlike, but the flight home was nothing short of a miracle and more proof of God's hand guiding me on this journey. Before we arrived at the airport, we stopped for lunch at a roadside taverna near the Canal of Corinth. Bev spotted a yiayia selling her handmade good luck charms and bought one. Made from wheat stalks woven in a spiral design with a tassel on the bottom, I thought they were ugly and teased Bev about wasting her money. "You can never have too much good luck," she laughed. Little did we know how right she was.

We had return tickets from Athens to the States on TWA flight #800. After arriving in New York, we boarded a plane for Seattle while Flight #800 took on passengers and headed for Paris. After only 13 minutes of flight time, the aircraft experienced an electrical failure, exploded, and fell from the sky into the Atlantic. More than 200 souls were lost. Back home in Vancouver, we did not learn of the crash until the next day. When we learned 13 minutes was the difference between living or dying, we were horrified and thankful. I have traveled to Greece several times since then, but Flight #800 still haunts me to this day.

I was right to worry my Greek family thought I was on flight #800, so I called Stathis as soon as I heard the news. He wept as he said, "I am so happy to hear you are safe. Surely God would not reunite our family only to have you die in a plane crash." Did that yiayia's charm have magical powers? I don't know, but superstition was a powerful force, and the coincidence *was* unsettling.

Back home for two months, Bev and I were shocked when an FBI agent came to our school to interview us. Unsure if the explosion was an act of terrorism or mechanical failure, the FBI was talking to every passenger on the Athens to New York flight. The first question the agent asked was my seat number on the plane, although I was sure he already knew. He asked me why I went to Greece, who I saw, and what I talked about when I was there. The oddest thing he asked was whether the bathrooms were out of order at any time during the flight. He said it was still early in the investigation, but NTSB officials thought the explosion had occurred in the fuel tank under the bathrooms. I told him no, the bathrooms were never out-of-order.

The extensive investigation concluded the tragedy of Flight #800 was caused by mechanical failure, not an act of terrorism. The news shook us to our core. On my next trip to Greece, I stopped at the Corinth taverna and saw the same yiayia selling her good luck charms. I bought one on the spot.

WHEN IT'S TIME TO
GO HOME

IT WAS THE SUMMER OF 2007, AND I WAS GLAD TO BE BACK in Greece after two years away. My usual itinerary involved spending a couple of days in Athens with my cousins before I took the bus to Hariklea's home in Patras. Finding my Nikolis family had blessed me with seven cousins who welcomed me with loving hearts and open arms. Raised on Lefkada, every cousin had moved to the mainland for school or work. Most made their home in Athens while Stathis attended school in Patras and lived with Hariklea's family. He enjoyed his year there, but the siren song of island life called to him, so he returned to Lefkada and opened his bakery.

Midmorning on my first day, we met at a beachfront coffee bar. The heat was already intense, but the breeze off the Mediterranean cooled us as we enjoyed our coffees. I was happy several of my cousins spoke English, making our conversations effortless as we caught up on each other's lives. After an hour, cousin Zoe, Thodoris' daughter, phoned Hariklea to tell her I had arrived and would see her on Monday.

I had an inkling something was up when their conversation lasted longer than what seemed necessary. Even so, I was not prepared for Zoe's announcement: "Maria, Hariklea has made other plans for your weekend. She wants you to come to Patras today."

"Why, today?" I asked.

"Because Hariklea wants to go home to her village and you are going to take her there," Zoe replied.

Her comment was met with dead silence. Then everyone was talking at once and peppering Zoe with questions. She quieted everyone down and continued: "Hariklea left Nikolis 44 years ago as a frightened, pregnant, teenager. Now she is an old woman who wants to see her childhood home one last time before she dies. When you arrive in Patras, she will rent a car for the drive to Lefkada. You will stay with Thodoris in his new house. Hariklea has even arranged for a translator during your visit." Retired and getting on in years, Zoe explained the brothers wanted their own homes. Their families had grown, and there were grandchildren now, so Thodoris had built a house in Agios Petros, the village nearest Nikolis.

Zoe's announcement caught me so off guard; it took a minute to realize the enormity of what Hariklea had requested. We sat in silence, each of us trying to get our heads around what this meant to the family when cousin Eve cut to the chase and stated, "Forty-four years ago your mother was forced to leave Nikolis because of you. Now 44 years later, she can return to Nikolis because of you." In two short sentences, Eve had articulated the irony of Hariklea's request. It was understandable and profound.

I finished my coffee, bid my cousins a hasty farewell, and promised to tell them everything when I returned to Athens on my way home. Cousin Stavros, Uncle Dimitri's son, pulled out his car keys and offered me a ride to the bus station. We stopped by my hotel so I could pick up my bags and cancel my reservation. Traffic was light, and we made good time to the bus station jam-packed with weekend travelers. With hugs and wishes for a good trip, Stavros and I parted ways. I bought a ticket and found a place to wait for the Patras bus.

What a crazy morning! In three hours, I had gone from sipping coffee on the beach to a hard, wooden, bench at a bus station. I had no idea what to expect, but the abrupt changes in my plans were small compared to the total transformation of my Greek family's life. All these changes only heightened my anticipation of the upcoming trip.

I boarded the bus for Patras and settled into my seat. Looking out the window at the familiar countryside, memories of my first visit to Lefkada in 1996 returned. With God's grace, a fork in the road and the letter "N," Bev and I had found tiny Nikolis clinging to a steep mountainside on our first day of looking. My uncles were more than a little shocked to meet the child Hariklea was carrying when she left the island. Hearing the grown woman standing in front of them was their niece must have been like seeing a ghost from the past. We shared a meal that started with a bit of tension but ended with Thodoris welcoming me to the family. Since then, I had made several trips to Nikolis where I helped by taking the goats out to pasture, feeding the livestock, and making feta cheese from goat's milk.

My thoughts were interrupted by the bus making a sharp turn as it pulled into the Patras station. I hailed a taxi to Hariklea's house where I walked in to find one suitcase sitting in the entry and Katina holding her baby boy. I guessed only two of us were going to Lefkada. I was humbled Hariklea chose me to fulfill her dream of returning to Nikolis, but I worried about Katina feeling left out. I was the new addition to the family, after all. As it turned out, I had fretted in vain because Katina had no intention of coming with us. She understood that with two young children and a husband to care for, she could not go.

Secretly, I was pleased only two of us were making this trip. Having Katina along would have made conversing easier, but returning to Nikolis was *our* story, and I sensed Hariklea felt the same way. Katina's husband drove us to downtown Patras, where we rented a small car with an anemic three-cylinder engine. Perfect for our duo, it suited the narrow roads and got good gas mileage. I laughed at the vehicle's splendid purple paint job, but I thought it was perfect for such a special occasion. That funny little car with its royal purple paint was the chariot that would deliver Hariklea back home. We stowed our bags and climbed in the car. Settled in, Hariklea looked at me and just said, "Pame" ("Let's go").

A WISH AND AN ANSWERED PRAYER

MY FIRST TASK WAS TO DRIVE TO THE NEARBY PORT, TAKE a car ferry across the Bay of Corinth and pick up the road for Lefkada. The boat cut hours off the drive but getting a car on board took professional driving skills and a rubber neck. These ferries were not opened on both ends, so I was forced to drive on board backward. Trying to avoid cars behind me and on both sides, while dock workers screamed "speed it up" was nerve-racking. I got the car on board without any body damage, but we were packed together so tightly, we couldn't open the doors and had to stay in our seats for the crossing. I was thankful the water was calm that day, and the trip across the bay was quick. Happy to be back on land, I pointed the car north, and we were off.

Driving together for hours with an unavoidable language barrier made for a challenging trip. We managed to converse about simple things, and while there was not much said, a lot was communicated. Barreling down the road, I wondered what could be more reasonable than a mother and daughter driving home to visit the relatives. Nothing, except we were no ordinary mother and daughter, and the home had remained unseen for four decades. The significance of what we were doing was not lost on us at all.

Entering the countryside, a two-lane road led us past endless farm fields and small lakes. All along the way, old trucks spewed thick black clouds as they labored under huge loads of beets, tobacco, melons, and tomatoes. The road was decent, but the traffic made for slow going. My map said the drive from Patras to Nikolis was three hours, but now I understood why the Greeks had told me it was a five-hour trip. After a couple of hours in the car, Hariklea fell sound asleep. As I peeked at her, my heart hurt for all she had suffered, but also swelled with the enormous respect I felt for her. Hariklea had endured unimaginable tragedy in her life, but she had not let adversity defeat her. She was a brave and compassionate woman who wanted her homecoming to be about forgiveness and healing, not settling old scores or rehashing regrets.

When Hariklea awoke from her nap, I asked about stopping for lunch at a lakeside town along the way. She was silent but smiled as she handed me a slice of bread and a banana, finger food to eat while I drove. I laughed out loud at her thriftiness and desire to make good time. When I realized our only stops would be for gasoline, I regretted renting such a fuel-efficient car.

We reached the causeway connecting mainland Greece to Lefkada Island as the sun was setting. Driving south along the coast, we had just enough moonlight to guide us until we reached towns with brightly lit shops and restaurants filled with diners. By my clock, it was late, but I had forgotten 8:30 p.m. in Greece was like the middle of the afternoon back home. As often as I had been to this ancient land, I still could not get used to living on "Greek time." Continuing south, we came to the steep road that climbed into the foothills and led to Thodoris' home. Fifteen hairpin turns later we pulled into his driveway.

There were hugs and kisses all around as Uncle Thodoris and Marianna came out to greet us. Once inside, we were introduced to our translator, Kalliopy, a friend of Thodoris who hailed from Michigan. She rented a nearby summer home with her husband, and they became close friends with the Voukelatos'. Hariklea and I got settled in our room before joining the others at the kitchen table. We stayed up for hours talking, laughing, and drinking Thodoris' homemade red *krasi*. With Kalliopy there to translate, the evening had a natural flow. I don't remember what was said as much as how loved I felt. Thodoris sat beside me, told me he loved me, and held my hand the entire evening. He released his grip only when it was time to refill our wine glasses. I couldn't have asked for a better ending to a long day. Around midnight Kalliopy returned home, and we went to bed. Tomorrow was going to be another big day.

We were up the next morning sipping coffee when there was a knock at the door. I opened it to find a tiny, senior, man with his hands in his pockets, watery eyes and trembling lips. He was shaking as he asked to come in. The minute he saw Hariklea, he shuffled to her as fast as he could, embraced her and sobbed. Kalliopi explained his name was Andreas Adipas, a childhood friend from Nikolis. They sat close together on kitchen chairs, holding one another like old friends do and sharing their news. The tender scene unfolding in front of us brought everyone to tears. How sad these two friends had lost out on a lifetime of friendship. Andreas was the first villager to welcome Hariklea home, and that meant the news had spread: Hariklea Voukelatos was back on Lefkada.

The excitement in the house was palpable as we changed clothes and prepared to leave for Nikolis. We were all expected for lunch with Nikos and Zahareena. There were five of us, so Thodoris and Marianna led the way in his truck with Hariklea, Kalliopi, and me following behind in the purple chariot. The drive was short, but no one spoke

188

along the way. I wanted Hariklea to have time to prepare herself as we drove over the steep, windy, roads she had not seen since she was a teenager. We passed the field where her mother's dowry of nine olive trees still grew and the olive press our fathers had shared. I turned right at the sign that led travelers to either Nikolis or Manassi and within minutes parked in front of Hariklea's old home. From the outside, the white, two-story, stucco house had not changed. The grape arbor was laden with grapes and garlic strands, and geraniums still grew in clay pots around the patio. I doubted much had changed since Hariklea had lived here.

Nikos, who was out front waiting, helped Hariklea out of the car and greeted her tenderly. Zahareena followed, but soon returned to the kitchen to put the finishing touches on the lunch she was preparing. Nikos cradled his sister's arm and became her cane as he led her around the outside of her home. While the others relaxed on the patio, I took photographs of Hariklea as she opened the outdoor bread oven, fingered the oregano drying on the fence and stopped by the pens where, as a girl, she had fed the goats and chickens. Nikos suggested they return to the patio to rest for a bit, but Hariklea insisted on visiting the long-neglected cemetery.

She pushed open the old iron gate and made her way past white marble headstones dating back generations. It didn't take Hariklea long to find where her mother, Zoe, was buried. There for the first time; she saw her father's grave along the side of her mother's. Two thick, marble crosses marked their plot. After leaving Nikolis, she never saw her father alive again. Standing there resolute and silent, Hariklea looked at the grave of the man who believed no punishment was too harsh for the person who brought shame to his family. In his mind, he felt entirely justified in beating his disobedient wife to death and exiling his pregnant child. Hariklea kept her feelings to herself, but I sensed she was glad she had come. Maybe this visit had given her some closure or at least a small measure of peace.

Our final stop was the home that had been both Hariklea's sanctuary and the scene of her worst nightmare. The house was small with bedrooms upstairs and the kitchen and living room on the main floor. As she opened the door, I worried what demons awaited her inside. The kitchen was the same, but with a few upgrades: a new refrigerator, stove, and washing machine. Hariklea nodded her approval as she ran her fingers over the latest appliances, table, and countertop. Touching those things made returning home concrete for her. As Hariklea walked into the living room, she paused to cross herself in front of the religious icons but did not linger there. If any memories of that awful day returned, Hariklea's calm demeanor hid her feelings well. She made her way back to the kitchen where she sat at the table and basked in the sunlight streaming through the window. Hariklea could have sat there all day savoring the same view she had loved as a girl.

Resting a spell, she took her time before she headed back outside to sit on a bench. Her gaze wandered across the valley to the olive trees tended by her family since the 1800s and up the hill to where her neighbors had lived. The home of my father, Yiorgos, was within eyesight. As we sat there looking at his house, our minds filled with compelling truths. To Hariklea, Yiorgos was a rapist who had ruined her life, betrayed everyone, and fled Lefkada like a coward. To me, he was a rapist and a coward but also a piece of the puzzle I would never find. Here we were two victims of Yiorgos sitting together hand in hand outside his former home. We had survived him and gone on to live meaningful lives. Somehow, I doubted if he could say the same.

Hariklea's next comment, "Thank you, Maria, my death will be easier now because I have returned home," filled my heart with warmth and peace. Despite all she had been through, Hariklea was still determined to live life on her terms. I was honored to help her complete her wish. Hariklea, like Ellen, possessed a strong spirit, and I was fortunate to have not one, but two, strong and loving mothers.

Looking up the road past Yiorgos' house, I saw the first of several villagers walking to greet Hariklea. I joined the rest of the family on the patio and watched as friends she had known when she was a young girl welcomed her home. I never tired of watching Greeks and the demonstrative ways they expressed their feelings. With hands flying as they speak, lips kissing with abandon, and loud voices, they used their entire bodies to communicate. Hariklea seemed excited to see her friends and greeted them warmly. Though I nearly missed it, she even smiled a couple of times.

After the last villager left, Hariklea and I rested on the bench while Uncle Nikos and Zahareena prepared the table for lunch. They brought out hand-embroidered linens, china plates, and crystal glasses for the occasion. Because Hariklea was a family member, a less elegant setting would have sufficed. But honoring the return of a sister deserved something special. Every delicacy Zahareena had prepared was grown no more than a stone's throw away from where we stood. There was roasted chicken, *dolmades* (grape leaves stuffed with rice and meat), warm bread, and salad. The smells of village cooking filled the mountain air with delicious aromas.

As we all took our seats, I made sure I sat between Kalliopy, our translator, and Hariklea, because I didn't want to miss a thing. There were kind words and lavish compliments all around as we thanked our hosts for such an elegant table and delectable food. Before we began, Nikos poured everyone a glass of *his* red krasi, raised his glass and spoke, "Today my sister has returned home after many years away. Let us thank God for reuniting our family." His comments were brief but powerful. With our glasses raised, we toasted Hariklea and welcomed her home. Overwhelmed by such an outpouring of love, even stoic Hariklea could not hold back the liquid joy flowing down her cheeks.

She was home, and she was happy. Sharing this journey with her was one of the most joyful and meaningful moments of my life. Hariklea and I had literally and figuratively come full circle.

The food was delicious, the conversation was relaxed, and happiness lit up every face. Looking to my left, I noticed Hariklea had stopped eating and was deep in thought. The look on her face told me it was something important, and I suspected she was reflecting on the twists and turns her life had taken. Surely, she had not expected to see her brothers or home again. I hoped she was basking in the thrill of returning home after 44 years. It was a lot for Hariklea to handle, so I gave her plenty of time before I asked her to put her thoughts into words. "For years I used to say," she professed, "εγώ δεν έχω στον ήλιο μοίρα»: «I have no fate or fortune under the sun.» Her brother, Thodoris, who had instantly understood this very Greek expression, choked up again and grabbed her by the hand. "But now," Hariklea's face lit up: "Fortune has smiled on me, and my sunshine is back forever."

EPILOGUE - 2018

COUSIN STATHIS OPENED A THRIVING BAKERY IN VASILIKIS during the 1990s. They say he makes the best Kourabiethes (shortbread cookies with confectioner's sugar and almonds) on Lefkada. Since opening his bakery, Stathis has learned to say "good morning" in 12 languages.

Cancer took Mom, Ellen Pace, in 2004. She was 86. Not a day goes by I don't miss her.

Brother Richard turned his life around over 20 years ago. He is happy and lives with his wife in San Diego. I visit as often as I can.

Brother Michael, his wife, and daughter live in the Pacific Northwest. It is lovely having them so close.

Sister Deirdre is still estranged from the family.

A new bridge connecting Patras to northern Greece was completed in 2004 for the Olympic Games. It eliminated much of the ferry traffic and cut two hours off the drive from Patras to Lefkada.

I continue to visit Greece as often as possible, spending time with my family in Athens, Lefkada, and Patras. We enjoyed 34 years as a "complete" family.

In 2016, uncle Thodoris died. His wife, Marianna, still lives near Nikolis and his children live in Athens.

My Athens uncle, Dimitris, died in 2017. His wife, Niki, and children live in Athens.

Uncle Nikos and Zahareena still reside in Nikolis. They continue harvesting olives and living off the land. In recent years they opened "Litheria," an old-style restaurant, where diners can go into the kitchen and select their dinner from the stove top. "Litheria" overlooks the southern tip of Lefkada and is located across the street from the white-washed market and olive tree where I first met Stathis.

In May of 2018, I went back to the Patras City Hall to see Mr. Alivizatos and thank him for his precious gifts. Like me, he was moved as we discussed times past and our "historic" encounters. I am forever indebted to him for his help.

Katina tirelessly cared for Hariklea until she passed away in February of 2019. She was in her 80s, and I will miss her deeply.

After Hariklea's funeral, Katina called and told me she listed *two* daughters' names in the obituary, hers and mine. Her actions surprised and filled me with joy. My existence was unknown to most of Hariklea's friends and all her late husband's family. Katina's bravery left her with a lot of explaining to do but completed the family circle in Patras as well as Lefkada. She is her mother's daughter!

I am returning to Patras this spring, 2019, to conclude filming a documentary about the Greek orphans of the 1950s. It will also be my first visit to Hariklea's grave.